# HANDGUN BASICS

## Safety & Handling

Written by
Dave Matheny
For
The American Association of
Certified Firearms Instructors

Handgun Basics: Safety & Handling.

Published by American Associaton of Certified Firearms Instructors

Nothing contained in this book is to be considered as the rendering of legal advice for specific cases and readers are responsible for obtaining such advice from their own legal counsel. The reader's individual legal counsel must fully research original and current sources of authority. This book and any techniques, charts, forms or other sample documents are intended solely for educational and instructional purposes.

First Printing, August, 2005

Library of Congress Cataloguing-in-Publication Data

American Association of Certified Firearms Instructors, Inc.

ISBN 0-9741480-2-4

Handgun Basics: Safety & Handling.

Printed in the United States of America by The First Impression Group, 2700 Blue Water Road, Suite 450, Eagan MN 55121-1429 (651) 683-1125

Written by Dave Matheny

Cover by Oleg Volk

Design, layout, and typesetting by Aaron Friday.

Photos by Larry Nevin. Used by permission.

# TABLE OF CONTENTS

# INTRODUCTION

# What This Book Is All About

## Who this book is for

This book is for anyone who wants to understand the safety rules and the basic function of handguns. And, while there are many very good books on individual handguns, there has not been a basic safety and handling book written in a very long time. Today, handguns are enjoying increased popularity due to the vast majority of states allowing law-abiding, competent adults to carry them for personal protection. So, as handguns become more present and their use increases, so goes the need for basic training.

You don't need to be an experienced gun owner, or even have ever so much as held a firearm, to benefit from this book. For those with some experience, this book is a good reference and provides an opportunity to brush up on your safety and handling practices. For the beginner, this book will help keep you safe and help you to ask better questions about any particular handgun you may encounter.

For those who detest handguns, knowledge is power. A basic understanding of handguns may help you understand that their evolution continues to include new and better safety mechanisms.

This book is also for those people — a small number, we hope — who think that a handgun is fun and cool, and whose firearms education has come from the television or movies. We hope and expect to change their perspective.

## Who we are

The American Association of Certified Firearms Instructors (AACFI) provides outstanding training in firearms safety, storage, and basic firearms handling, as well as permit-to-carry and advanced defensive-carry instruction. We are dedicated to protecting, promoting and defending America's longstanding tradition of the safe and lawful use of privately owned firearms.

**Joseph E. Olson**, the President of AACFI, is Professor of Law at Hamline University and a long-time political activist involved in 2nd Amendment issues, as well as a former member of the board of directors of the National Rifle Association. A former federal prosecutor and experienced defense counsel, he is licensed to practice law in Minnesota and California. In addition to being an NRA Certified Firearms Instructor since 1985, Olson is a graduate of the Judicious Use of Deadly Force course, the Lethal Threat Management for Civilians course, and the LFI Refresher Course at the Lethal Force Institute. He has also graduated from the Tactical Pistol course at Gunsite Training Center, the Urban Rifle course at Thunder Ranch Training Center, the Advanced Pistolcraft course at Chapman Academy, the Arizona Concealed Carry course at the Urban Firearms Institute, and the Nevada Concealed Carry course at Armed and Safe, Inc. Olson has been issued carry permits in Arizona, Florida, Maine, Massachusetts, Minnesota, New Hampshire, and Washington state. Olson is the President of the American Association of Certified Firearms Instructors, an organization dedicated to training civilians not only on the laws and technicalities related to carrying a handgun for personal protection, but also on strategies and tactics to avoid the need to use a handgun for personal protection. Mr. Olson holds Counselor, Certifier, and Instructor ratings from AACFI.

**Tim Fleming Grant**, the Vice President of AACFI, is a political activist and marketing professional. Grant's interest in firearms and self-defense began in February of 1996 when his cousin was killed in a drive-by shooting in Golden Valley, Minnesota. Grant holds an MBA from the University of St. Thomas, graduate credits from St. Paul Seminary, and a Bachelor of Arts degree in Political Science and Economics from the

University of Minnesota. He also holds both Instructor and Certifier ratings from AACFI.

For this book, there are others to thank for their expertise and contribution to style and accessibility.

**Bryan Phillips** is an airline pilot and composer of music with an elaborate recording studio in his home. Bryan is also a gun collector extraordinaire and a passionate collector of firearms information. He is a certified firearms instructor for the NRA and AACFI, a gunsmith, and a former handgun competitor. He has also attended extensive law-enforcement training classes.

**Teresa J. Reiter** is an NRA Practical Pistol Instructor, NRA Eddie Eagle advocate, Minnesota Department of Natural Resources Firearms Safety Instructor, and longtime firearms instructor who developed and specializes in "Introductory Firearms for Women" classes. She is also founder and CEO of TJ's Firearms Training, Inc., and an AACFI instructor. Teresa, having instructed so many women who were complete newcomers to shooting, was our bridge to that half of the world that knows almost nothing about guns. Her contributions were invaluable.

**Steve Morin** explains: "By trade, I am a machinist in the medical science periphery. That's where my technical background on firearms gets its impetus, and I enjoy working on guns just for the fun of tinkering." He is state-certified to teach the Minnesota Firearm Safety Hunter Education course, has been an active instructor for seven years, and is serving his second term as Vice President of the Minnesota Firearm Safety Instructors Association. He is also NRA-certified as both a range safety officer and a basic home firearm safety, pistol, and rifle instructor.

## Orientation

Let's start at the beginning. When developing the AACFI's Basic Handgun Training Course and this book, we did a lot of reading and research, and found that very little updating of basic handgun training had been done. Individual instructors may have stayed abreast of changes in technology, laws or safety practice developments over the last 25 years, but we could not find anyone who had done it in an organized way for beginners.

Whether or not you continue your firearms training or maybe even apply for a permit to carry, learning the basics about firearms is like learning CPR or first aid. It's a skill that will remain with you should it be needed. You don't need to go out and buy a handgun; you don't even have to like handguns. Knowing about them and how they work is valuable in its own right. It may help you save a life. "Forewarned is forearmed" is an age old adage that applies exceedingly well to firearms and handgun training. Our goal is to make handgun training accessible, current, interesting and fun. Our classes will take a multimedia approach, and provide a hands-on shooting opportunity in a safe and comfortable environment.

Far too many people, including some who have owned guns all of their lives, have picked up misinformation from television and newspapers. We hope to clear up the misinformation out there. That's what this book is all about.

## Humor

Dealing with handguns on the range, in the woods, or at home is a serious matter and must be taken seriously. That doesn't mean a little humor every now and then is a bad idea. In fact, we think it's essential, and we hope that the occasional touches of humor in this book are appreciated and not misunderstood.

There are, however, things we don't joke about. One of them is pointing a handgun at a human being. Another topic that we find utterly unfit for jokes is safety issues involving the handling of firearms.

## Keeping it simple

We believe in keeping things simple whenever possible. There are sound psychological, legal, and physiological reasons for this. We want you to enjoy learning about firearms safety and shooting. Leveraging that which comes naturally to us, as humans, will only make our learning experiences better.

That doesn't mean that we've oversimplified issues. Some of the matters touched upon in this book are complicated, and while we've tried to boil them down, the simple truth is that anything involving handguns, the law or human behavior isn't simple. We've tried to strike a balance here.

*Safety is your responsibility.*

# CHAPTER 1
## How Handguns Work

The modern handgun comes close to being a perfect piece of machinery. A well-made
gun, and most of them are, will perform the
job of propelling a bullet downrange at great
speed many thousands of times. Rarely, if
ever, will it fail to function. If it does, the reason will almost certainly be that the owner
failed to maintain it properly.

Modern handguns will last for decades, maybe even centuries, if
properly maintained. In fact, they are so well designed and so very well
made that we don't know how long a well-cared-for handgun *will* last.

It's never wise to say that a particular technology has gone as far as
it can—history has a way of making fools out of those who say that sort

of thing—but the fact is that there have been
no major innovations in handguns for about a
century. There have been improvements,
however, largely through better materials and
manufacturing methods, along with refine-
ments here and there.

A gun-familiar Rip Van Winkle who awoke today after having been
asleep since the early 1900s might have trouble grasping all of the other

changes that have taken place in the world, from space travel to cell phones, from open-heart surgery to the Internet, but he could pick up a modern semiautomatic pistol or revolver and know exactly how to load and shoot it.

He would be astonished at the lightness of some modern handguns, and might need a small amount of coaching to disassemble a particular pistol. Otherwise, he would be right at home with this one aspect of today's technology.

Most of the past 100 years has been spent simply perfecting the handgun.

## How we got here: market forces

Guns are manufactured the way they are today because, through the centuries, shooters have demanded ever greater accuracy, safety, reliability, efficiency and convenience.

The earliest guns of the 1300s, some of which had barrels made of wood bound with iron hoops, were fiendishly inconvenient to shoot, as well as dangerous to their users. They had to be fired by plunging the end of a smoldering rope into a touch-hole. Even then, they often didn't fire. When they did, they frequently blew up in shooters' faces. Those earliest guns would have gotten a horrible review from any 14th Century consumer advocate.

By the late 1700s, about the time of our Revolutionary War, handguns, as well as long guns, had become fairly reliable and far less hazardous to shooters. Nevertheless, they were still

**Figure 1**

unsatisfactory. The state of the art by then had advanced to the flintlock (Figure 1). When you pulled the trigger, the hammer, which carried a piece of flint, fell and struck sparks into a pan containing a small amount of powder. The burning powder's flame travels through a small hole in the barrel and ignites the main charge, sending the projectile (a small lead ball) on its way.

A fever was driving handgun development: the desire for a repeating gun. Think of pirates with several pistols tucked into their belts. This was an early attempt to achieve increased firepower.

By 1800, a handgun could still fire just once (once per barrel, anyway) each time it was loaded. Gun makers tried putting two, three, four, or more barrels on a gun, but that was a clumsy solution. They still required a maddeningly slow reloading process involving a ramrod, powder, ball, and priming.

If you had many pistols, you could fire several shots as fast as you could drop one gun and grab another. But that was not very fast, and there was the expense of owning all those guns.

## The repeater

By the 1830s, Samuel Colt was selling a repeating revolver that could fire six times with only a brief pause between shots for the thumb to re-cock the hammer (Figure 2). Shooters now had their repeating gun, but they were still not satisfied. After all six shots were fired, there was the same, slow and tedious reloading process involving the ramrod, powder, ball, and primer.

**Figure 2**

Inventors remained at their drawing boards and eventually came up with an all-in-one metal package: bullet in the front, powder inside, primer on the back.

## The cartridge solution

By the 1870s, you could flick open a gate at the back of the cylinder, drop in six of these new "cartridges," as they were called, and get back to shooting.

Still, shooters were not satisfied. They had to thumb-cock the hammer between shots, which slowed them down, although you'd never guess that from Western movies.

## Dawn of the double-action

In the late 1870's, a new kind of revolver was invented. You could either thumb-cock it the old way, or just use your forefinger to pull the trigger through a long, heavy pull. The long trigger pull would rotate the cylinder, bringing a fresh cartridge in line with the barrel, cock the hammer and, at the end of the pull, drop the hammer and fire the gun.

Linguistic confusion began at about this point. The old kind of revolver could only be fired one way: by first cocking and then pulling the trigger. It was called a "single-action" because the trigger performed only one action—releasing the hammer.

**Figure 3**

The new revolver had a trigger that performed two actions, both cocking and releasing the hammer, so it was called the "double-action." (See Figure 3.)

What makes it confusing is that the gun requiring two steps is called the "single-action", and the one that can be cocked and fired in just one step is called the "double-action." Just remember that single-action and double-action refer to the number of actions the *trigger* performs.

But, of course, handgunners were still not satisfied. Now they were complaining that reloading was too slow. The military in particular wanted rapid reloading, and military contracts are enormously important to gun makers. Not only does the military order guns by the hundreds of thousands, many civilians want whatever the military has, so a military contract is a hole-in-one for a gun maker.

Rapidly reloading a revolver was impossible. A cavalryman at a gallop was more likely to spill cartridges in the sagebrush than get them into the gun. Also, when it came to accurate shooting, the short, light trigger pull of the single-action was preferable to the long, heavy pull of the double-action.

## The semiautomatic

By the 1890s, gun designers had provided an answer: the self-loading pistol[1], or semiautomatic (Figure 4). (In this book, we call this type of handgun a "semiauto.") This design used the energy generated by the fired cartridge (or round) to reload a round in the chamber of the gun. That energy removed and ejected the spent case from the chamber, cocked the hammer, and picked up and chambered a new cartridge from a magazine full of replacements. (This process is described in detail on

**Figure 4**

---

[1] *Handgun* refers to all types of guns designed to be held and fired with one hand, while *revolver* refers to a handgun with a rotating cylinder. *Pistol* and *semiautomatic* refer to semiautomatic, or "semiauto," handguns—those with a detachable magazine.

page 21.)

All the rounds could easily be fired in a couple of seconds, and the semiauto could be reloaded in a flash by inserting a fresh, loaded magazine. Firing could be resumed with little interruption. A charging cavalryman could shoot rapidly, as long as he had loaded magazines. And yes, odd as it sounds today, the cavalry was a big market for semiautos as the 20th Century began.

There were attempts to keep the revolver competitive in the rapid-fire field. One was to use a "top-break" revolver (Figure 5). It ejected all the cases when opened by slamming it across a cavalryman's thigh. Fresh cartridges could be dropped in with the free hand, and the revolver closed with a flick of the wrist. That was a good idea that never quite caught on, possibly because it required a lot more dexterity than the average trooper or cavalryman was likely to have. On the other hand, the military saw how easy it would be to train its people to use the semiauto (i.e., drop the empty magazine and slam in a new one), and the semiauto was here to stay.

**Figure 5**

## Browning's guns

No description of modern gun development would be complete without at least a mention of the most influential gun designer who ever lived, John M. Browning (Figure 6). Born in 1855, he produced over 50 designs in his lifetime, with over 20 of them being commercially produced in large quantities. Browning's designs, with only minor modifications, still dominate small arms across the world.

In 1911, the U.S. military accepted Browning's design for a semiauto pistol, the Colt .45 Auto, also called the "Government Model" or the "1911"

**Figure 6**

(Figure 7). Almost all semiautos made today are versions of it, and the 1911 design itself, with minor modifications, is still made or copied around the world in vast numbers. As the grand-daddy of semiautos, we will use it (or copies of it) as our semiauto example in this book.

**Figure 7**

## Today's market

There are other, less well-known handgun types, including single-shot handguns, such as the Thompson Contender, and some bolt-action designs. Flintlock and cap-and-ball handguns are still made as historic reproductions.

The two main handgun types, revolver and semiauto, have virtually dominated the handgun market for the past century. As we said in *Chapter 1*, there seems to be little room for major innovation in either of these types of handguns today, although minor improvements have been made here and there.

At this point, we can describe how they work without fear that some new handgun is going to sweep all existing gun designs into the dumpster.

## The parts of a handgun

Traditionally, the major components of a handgun have been described as the barrel, frame, and action. Tradition has its place, but because revolvers and semiautos differ in so many ways, we'll very soon come to a fork in the road in discussing gun parts. That said, parts such as the trigger, trigger guard, and
grip are common to both types of handguns and are well-known enough to need little in the way of description at this point. But another part that the revolver and semiauto have in common—the barrel—is more complicated than it appears at first and can be looked at closely here.

### Barrel

The *barrel* is a tube made of extremely strong steel. The inside of the tube, the *bore*, is rifled, which means it has grooves carefully machined into it. If you look down a barrel (of a disassembled gun, for safety's sake), you will see spiral grooves. (All James Bond movies begin with a view down a rifled barrel.) The end of the barrel, where the bullet exits, is called the *muzzle*. See Appendix A for a cutaway diagram of a handgun.

The raised, plateau-like parts of the rifling are called *lands*, and the low parts are called *grooves*. Their job is to bite into the relatively soft bullet as it travels down the bore, making it spin. This spin is not unlike the spin a quarterback puts on a football when he throws a pass. As with a football, the spin stabilizes a bullet through its flight.

## Frame

The *frame* of the handgun includes the grip, where you hold the gun, the trigger guard, and the supporting structure for the barrel and the ammunition supply (the *cylinder* of a revolver and the *magazine* of a semi-auto). The frame also houses the components of the *action*. A revolver's frame looks very different than a semiauto's. We'll discuss the differences when we talk about each type of handgun. At this point, just remember that the frame brings it all together, like a bike frame brings together the steering mechanism, wheels, pedals and chain drive of a bicycle. Without the frame, you would have nothing.

Frames can be made of a variety of materials. Traditionally, they are made of steel. Today, frames are manufactured from a number of different metals or polymers, from aluminum to plastics. In general, new materials have been introduced to make handguns lighter.

## Action

The *action* includes all of the parts needed to make the gun fire a cartridge. The action begins with the trigger and ends with the firing pin. Within the action are a number of components including springs, levers, and safety mechanisms. The action of a revolver differs greatly from that of a semiauto. Each will be discussed in turn. The working mechanism of the action and safety mechanism is where new ideas and modifications to handguns have taken place and continue to take place.

We have touched upon "single-action" and "double-action" revolvers. For now, we know that these represent the mechanisms that fire the handgun.

And here we come to the fork in the road.

## Revolver

**Figure 8**

The revolver's most notable feature, from which it derives its name, is the revolving cylinder that holds the cartridges in individual chambers (Figure 8). The idea of having several loaded chambers arranged in a circle, each one ready to fire, goes back a couple of hundred years. The design is still hard to beat for its simplicity.

The cylinder is revolved either by the hammer being pulled back (in the single-action revolver) or by the trigger being pulled (in the double-action revolver). In either case, the shooter's hand provides the power to present a new cartridge and take the old one away.

**Figure 9**

Most cylinders have six chambers, thus the Old West term *six-gun* (Figure 9). Some have more (usually guns with lighter, smaller cartridges, such as the .22 rimfire), while some have only four or five chambers (usually those with heftier cartridges, or small guns for which compactness is important).

To review, in the single-action (SA) revolver, thumb-cocking the hammer rotates the cylinder, bringing a fresh cartridge in line with the barrel. Double-action (DA) revolvers are cocked either by thumb-cocking the hammer or by the forefinger pulling the trigger back.

Some revolvers have hidden hammers and can be fired only by pulling the trigger (Figure 10). These revolvers are called double-action only (DAO).

**Figure 10**

In both cases, the mechanism that rotates the cylinder is fairly complicated. **Note**: The mechanism is located behind an access plate, and any work on it should be left to a gunsmith.

The cylinder is housed in a rectangular cutout inside the frame (Figure 11). The frame also houses moving parts such as the trigger, the hammer, and a mechanical device called the "hand." The hand rotates the cylinder so the fired cartridge is moved away and a fresh one presented for each shot.

**Figure 11**

The grip is also part of the frame (Figure 12). On most revolvers, the wood or synthetic grips may be changed to better fit the owner's hand and preferences. Grips come in a variety of sizes and materials.

**Figure 12**

## Revolver firing cycle

What happens when a revolver is fired is much the same in both single- and double-action revolvers. We will illustrate what goes on from the moment the hammer falls, using a modern Smith & Wesson model 65 double-action revolver (Figure 13) as an example. (The fact that this gun is a double-action makes no difference for this illustration, since what happens from the moment the hammer begins to fall is exactly the same in both double-action and single-action revolvers.)

**Figure 13**

1. The hammer falls and strikes the firing pin, which strikes the primer of the cartridge with great force.

2. The primer, which is filled with a chemical that reacts to the crushing blow, spews sparks, which ignite the propellant inside the cartridge case.

3. The propellant burns rapidly, creating tremendous pressure inside the cartridge case, which, in turn, expands against the walls of the chamber. The chamber wall and the breech face behind the cartridge momentarily trap this tremendous surge of energy.

4. The bullet, which is only lightly secured inside the cartridge, cannot resist the pressure for long. The tremendous energy of the expanding gas forces the bullet to depart the case. The bullet travels through the chamber mouth and enters the forcing cone (a funnel-shaped area at the back of the barrel designed to catch the bullet).

5. Guided by the forcing cone, the bullet continues its travel and enters the barrel itself, contacts the lands and grooves of the bore, and begins spinning.

6. A tiny amount of the expanding gas escapes at the barrel-cylinder gap. Most of the gas is not allowed to go anywhere but down the bore. For the moment, the brass case has inflated and

is closing off the back end of the chamber. (Technically, this is called *obturation*. If obturation didn't happen, there would be less pressure, bullets would move a lot slower, and shooters would be subjected to a highly unpleasant spray of superheated gas.)

7.  Because the gun is so much heavier than the bullet, the gun doesn't recoil significantly until the bullet has left the bore.

It's very simple. To fire this double-action gun again, the shooter will have to release the trigger, which will retract the hammer and firing pin behind the breech face, and re-engage the firing mechanism. When the trigger is pulled again, or when the hammer is thumb-cocked, the cylinder will rotate and bring another chamber into position, so the gun can fire again.

## Single-action revolvers

In the case of a single-action revolver, such as a Ruger Vaquero (a cowboy-style revolver, Figure 14), the hammer is drawn back by the thumb to cock the gun. Remember, its single-action name comes from the trigger's ability to do just one thing: release the hammer.

**Figure 14**

Besides being a single-action revolver, we chose the Vaquero as our example for another reason. Like all recent Ruger revolvers, a different method is used to strike the cartridge's primer. The hammer has no fir-

**Figure 15**

ing pin. Instead, the gun uses a *transfer bar* to enhance safety (Figure 15). The transfer bar transmits the energy of the hammer blow to an internal frame-mounted firing pin. It is similar to what happens when a croquet player puts a foot on top of a ball that's resting against another ball, and strikes the one under foot with the mallet. The energy is transferred, even though the mallet (in our case, the hammer) never comes into direct contact with the second ball (or firing pin).

Ruger is not the only gun maker to use the transfer bar principle. Transfer bars work well as safety mechanisms on single-action revolvers, because the trigger rebound (the distance the trigger travels forward when it is released after firing) is only a fraction of the double-action trigger. There is not enough forward movement on single-action's trigger to retract the hammer, but there is enough travel to retract a transfer bar out of the way. As the transfer bar drops out of its firing position, the firing pin retreats back into the frame. That is, when the trigger is pulled to the rear, the last fraction of an inch of trigger movement moves the transfer bar to make the connection between the hammer and the firing pin. When the trigger is released, the transfer bar retreats from its firing position. That way, if the gun is dropped on the hammer (whether it is cocked or not), the hammer should harmlessly hit the frame and not the firing pin.

## Double-action revolvers

Much of how single-action revolvers fire is shared by double-action revolvers. However, the way in which cartridges are readied for firing is different, as is the way the firing pin retracts once the trigger is released.

Double-action revolvers do not require manually cocking the hammer, although almost all still allow for this to be done. The longer and heavier trigger pull rotates the cylinder and cocks the hammer. At the

very end of the trigger pull, the hammer releases and fires the cartridge. Double-action revolvers that allow for manually cocking the hammer are (as a matter of action identification) called double-action, single-action revolvers (DA/SA).

As with a single-action revolver, the trigger rebound operates a safety mechanism. For the double-action revolver, this is called the *rebound slide*. The slide retracts the hammer and pushes the hammer block up between the frame and hammer. As the hammer retracts, it allows the firing pin to retract. The hammer block will keep the hammer from accidentally striking the firing pin. The rebound slide also locks the hammer in place until the trigger is pulled again.

## DAO revolvers

Double-action only (DAO) revolvers have been around for over a century (Smith & Wesson offered one to the Army in 1889). The vast majority are "hammerless," which means the hammer is enclosed inside the frame (Figure 16). A somewhat similar effect can be achieved by having a gunsmith grind off the hammer spur, making it difficult to thumb-

**Figure 16**

cock the gun and unlikely to catch on clothing. This modification, called "bobbing the hammer," should be undertaken only by a gunsmith.

Hammerless and "bobbed-hammer" revolvers are less likely to catch on clothing because the hammer spur doesn't project. This makes unintended firings far less likely. The DAO action is desired for its added safety. As with almost any handgun characteristic, there are tradeoffs. The double-action trigger pull is long and heavy and does not lend itself to highly accurate shooting.

## Semiauto

Even the barrel of the semiauto (Figure 17) is different from that of a revolver. The revolver's chamber is contained in the cylinder. The cartridge case being slightly larger than the bullet, the chamber has to be slightly larger in diameter than the bore. The semi-

**Figure 17**

auto's chamber is inside the back end of the barrel. It is fortified with walls thicker than the barrel. Additionally, in many semiautos, the barrel "floats" inside the slide and is secured only when the handgun is in battery[2] and ready to fire.

During firing, pressures soar inside the cartridge case, which is a frail brass cylinder. The chamber's job, just as in the revolver, is to control that energy and direct it toward pushing the bullet down the bore. That's why the chamber end is usually enlarged on the outside for additional strength.

Now we come to the rest of the gun. Our narrative could run right off the road and into a bewildering array of complexity if we tried to de-

---

[2] Being in battery is when a cartridge is chambered, and the slide has locked the barrel with the chamber into a fire-ready position.

scribe the functioning of every kind of semiauto there is; there are so many configurations.

**Figure 18**

We will start with a basic semiauto handgun, the Browning-designed Model 1911 Colt .45 Auto (Figure 18). As mentioned above, its operating system forms the basis of almost every semiauto made. There have been many small improvements, but this pistol is the great granddaddy of them all.

We start with the barrel. It is nestled inside the *slide*[3], and the slide sits on the frame. The slide and frame are mated to each other by a set of *rails*. The rails guide the slide as it moves forward and backward during the firing cycle. The lower part of the frame is the grip, which you hold in your hand. The upper portion of the frame contains the trigger, trigger guard, and some mechanical devices we'll discuss later. See *Appendix A* for a cutaway diagram of a semiauto.

## Semiauto firing cycle

The Colt model 1911 has been replicated by a number of different manufacturers, so its firing process is well known. Let's go through its firing cycle in sequence and explain each part and what it does. If some of the following sounds familiar, it's because some of the actions occurring inside a semiauto are much like those that occur inside a revolver.

**Figure 19**

We'll start with a gun that has a round in the chamber and is cocked — that is, the hammer has been pulled back against spring pressure (Figure 19). Remember that a semiauto's chamber is integrated into the rear of the barrel. A notch on the underside of the hammer is being

---

[3] The slide of a semiauto contains the locking system of the breech and components of the action, including the firing pin. It rides on rails manufactured into the top of the frame and accommodates the barrel. It also contains the following parts or assemblies:

- The breech face and locking mechanism with the chamber
- The firing pin and firing pin spring
- The extractor claw and spring to extract the spent case
- The recoil spring and rod
- One or more safety mechanisms and additional elements of the action, depending on the make and model of the firearm

engaged by the *sear*, a small piece of metal that releases the hammer when the trigger is pulled. The mainspring pushes against the hammer while the sear holds it. When the trigger is pulled, it moves the sear until the hammer slips off its notch.

At this point, let's follow events in extreme slow motion. What happens now is so fast that it is over before the human eye can register it.

1. The hammer falls and strikes the firing pin.

2. The primer, filled with a chemical that reacts to the crushing blow, spews sparks that ignite the propellant inside the cartridge case.

3. The propellant burns rapidly, creating tremendous pressure inside the cartridge case, expanding it against the walls of the chamber.

4. The case is effectively held inside the chamber for an instant by the pressure of expanding gasses. Because the bullet is only lightly secured inside the case, and because the chamber and the breech face are strong, nothing moves but the bullet. In short, it moves in response to the transfer of energy generated by the expanding gas and burning propellant.

5. The bullet starts traveling down the bore and contacts the lands and grooves, which cause it to spin. Expanding gasses are not allowed to go anywhere but down the bore.

6. About the time the bullet leaves the muzzle, the slide and barrel, which have temporarily mated the chamber (at the back of the barrel) and frame into battery, begin moving backwards in recoil.

7. After the slide has traveled about 1/10 of an inch, a link attached to the underside of the barrel pulls it down and out of the way, disengaging it from the slide.

8. The slide continues rearward and rides over the *disconnector*, which disengages the sear from the rest of the trigger mechanism and re-engages it with the hammer. It is this step that keeps the handgun from becoming a fully automatic firearm.

9. The spent case is connected to the slide by a small claw, called the *extractor*, which is hooked into

the extractor groove on the case. As the slide continues rearward and separates from the barrel, the claw draws the spent case out of the chamber. The extractor claw pulls the case backward, free of the chamber.

10. At this point, the case head encounters a small metal part on the frame, called the *ejector*. This very simple part's only job is to direct the spent case out the ejector port.

11. The slide continues rearward, compressing the recoil spring. It also pushes the hammer back and cocks it.

12. The slide has now accomplished everything it can by recoiling. In the next instant, it reaches the farthest point in its rearward travel. The big recoil spring now pushes it forward.

13. The breech face on the slide encounters the upper edge of the next cartridge at the top of the stack inside the magazine and pushes it forward.

14. Pushed by the slide, the cartridge slips forward out of the magazine. The bullet encounters a very short ramp that guides it into the chamber. The back end of the cartridge, the base, slides up the breech face, and the extractor claw engages the extractor groove of the cartridge case.

15. A millisecond later, the breech closes and the barrel and slide are again mated together securely. The fresh cartridge is sealed inside the chamber, the extractor claw is engaged, and the hammer is cocked. The gun is once again in battery. Once the shooter releases the trigger to go forward, it re-engages the sear with the trigger mechanism, and the gun can be fired again.

16. When the last cartridge is fired, the follower (the spring cover on which the cartridges rest while in the magazine) pushes up on the slide stop, locking the slide open. After removing the empty magazine and inserting a loaded one, the shooter will have to pull the slide back slightly or push the slide stop lever down to release the slide. The slide then slams forward, chambering a cartridge.

17. The gun can now be fired again.

## Semiauto variants

There are several variations on the basic semiauto. They do not change the basic chambering, firing and discharging of the cartridge. Rather, they are examples of modifications made in hopes of improving the basic function.

**Figure 20**

The Browning-designed Colt described here has a particular method of mating the barrel to the chamber. A row of large, rib-like projections on the top of the chamber end of the barrel engages a row of similar ribs on the inside of the slide (Figure 20). (The two are mated only temporarily. This ends when the link pulls the barrel away during of recoil.)

A modern variant is for the top of the chamber end of the barrel to be formed into a large block (Figure 21). The block is engaged by the ejection port itself, thus accomplishing the same temporary union that the Browning's interlocking ribs achieved.

**Figure 21**

Browning himself modernized the 1911 design in the 1920s with the 9mm pistol that came to be known as the Browning High Power. Among other things, he eliminated the link. The barrel is pulled away from the recoiling slide: a ramp milled into the underside of the barrel slides along a bar attached to the underside of the frame. This was a simpler, better solution, with fewer moving parts. Virtually all modern semiauto designs, other than the 1911, use the simplified system.

## Sidebar: Other methods of semiauto operation

The above is a description of a *recoil-operated semiauto*, which means the gun uses the force of the recoiling slide to power its cycle: open, eject, cock, chamber new cartridge, and close. Most handguns of 9mm and larger cartridges are recoil-operated.

**Figure 22**

The second common type of semiauto operation is *blowback* (Figure 22). The cycle of the blowback is very similar, but the barrel stays in place, locked to the frame, while the slide moves (Figure 23). At first, the spent case remains inside, effectively glued to the chamber by expansion under pressure. A

**Figure 23**

millisecond after firing, the case contracts slightly. The force of the cartridge explosion "blows back" the cartridge casing, driving the slide backward. Otherwise, the operation is very much the same as a recoil-operated action.

Blowback actions are commonly found on guns of somewhat lighter caliber, typically the .380 ACP and smaller. There are exceptions, however. The Thompson submachine gun of .45 ACP used a blowback system.

In a few cases, such as the Desert Eagle, the slide is gas-operated. A small amount of the gas generated by the firing is siphoned away from inside the bore and used to cycle the slide.

## Sidebar: The disconnector

The semiauto firing sequence happens so fast that the shooter has no time to release the trigger before the firing cycle is complete. You would be justified in asking why the gun doesn't fire again—and again, and again.

In other words, why doesn't the semiauto turn into a full auto?

The designers of the earliest semiautos foresaw this problem way back in the 1890s, and all semiautos are provided with a device called a *disconnector*. The trigger is disconnected from the firing mechanism until the shooter allows the trigger to travel forward. With the trigger disconnected, the hammer is reset but will not drop onto the firing pin until the trigger is reset and pulled again. Also, the firing pin is spring operated. The firing pin spring keeps the firing pin from flying forward as the slide travels forward. Were the firing pin not secured, it might well fire another shot, or series of shots. Such a dangerous condition is known as a "slam fire." Any semiauto that fires more than one shot with a single pull of the trigger is dangerous and illegal. Stop firing it immediately, unload it, and take the gun to a gunsmith.

**Figure 24**

To check the disconnector, first verify that the gun is unloaded. Then, pointing the gun in a safe direction, move the slide back about a quarter of an inch and pull the trigger (Figure 24). If the disconnector is working properly, the firing mechanism will not function.

In addition to the firing pin spring, a system pioneered during the 1970s locks the firing pin and automatically unlocks it only when the trigger is pulled the last fraction of an inch during its most rearward travel. This passive internal safety system is used on almost all semiautos today.

So there you have the semiauto's firing cycle at its most basic. Most modern semiautos are provided with several other features:

**Magazine release** (Figure 25): Usually a short lever or button on the left side of the frame, near where the trigger guard meets the grip. Some semiautos, generally smaller ones or those of lighter calibers, have magazine releases in the form of sliding catches on the underside (butt) of the grip.

**Figure 25**

**Figure 26**

**Safety** (Figure 26): External safeties (if the firearm is equipped with one) are usually, but not always, mounted high on the left side above the grip panel, either on the frame or the slide. Check the owner's manual.

Safeties are discussed at length in *Chapter 3*, but it's enough to say here that any safety is merely intended to keep the gun from firing. The key word here is *intended*. Any safety can malfunction and not prevent firing, and no shooter should ever depend on the safety.

Put another way, if the safety is the only thing preventing you from shooting something you did not want to shoot, you are not handling the gun safely.

**De-cocking lever** (Figure 27): A lever found on some semiautos that safely lowers or un-cocks the hammer, even though the chamber may be loaded. It is generally located on the side of the slide or the frame and may include a safety position that also disables the firing mechanism.

**Figure 27**

**Figure 28**

**Takedown lever** (Figure 28): On most semiautos, a lever or button protrudes from the left side of the frame. It is used to disassemble the gun. The owner's manual will provide detailed instructions for disassembly.

## A note on magazines

Magazines hold cartridges to be loaded into the chamber. They typically come in two styles (Figure 29). A single stack magazine has the cartridges sit directly on top of each other. A double stack holds the cartridges in two offset, staggered columns. The double stack typically holds more rounds. With the expiration of the 1994 Assault Weapons Ban, new magazines can once again be manufactured for civilian sales that hold more than the maximum 10 rounds allowed under the ban.

**Figure 29**

*Always check your owner's manual for instructions for your particular handgun.*

## Sidebar: Double-action semiauto

The Browning-designed Colt 1911 described above is, as we said, the prototype of all modern semiautos. But its offspring include some important modern variants. The 1911 is described as a single-action gun — even though it is not a revolver — because its trigger has no function other than to release the hammer. A common variant is the double-action/single-action (DA/SA) semiauto. Like many revolvers, semiautos can have several firing modes.

**Figure 30**

The first double-action semiauto appears to have been the Walther P38, a German design dating back to World War II (Figure 30). It was designed so that the shooter could chamber a round and then use a decocker to lower the hammer without firing the gun. The shooter could then carry it in the same manner and with the same sense of security that he or she could carry a double-action revolver — with the hammer down and a round in the chamber.

It could then be fired with a long, heavy trigger pull, just like a double-action revolver. All successive shots are fired with the usual lighter and shorter single-action trigger pull.

## Sidebar: Striker-fire semiauto

Striker-fire semiautos appeared around the start of the 20th Century. The Luger, for example, is a recoil-operated semiauto with, at the time of its introduction, an unusual firing mechanism. The firing pin is part of a larger plunger, which is held in place under spring tension until released by trigger movement. This semiauto is hammerless and has a trigger pull similar to a single-action revolver.

Today, striker-fire semiautos have trigger pulls that vary widely in length and weight. Striker actions are still technically single- or double-action firing mechanisms, even though their design differs significantly from traditional hammer-style firing mechanisms. It depends on whether the trigger pull cocks and releases the plunger, or just releases it. From the shooter's perspective, striker-fire semiautos have the same trigger pull for every round fired. A heavier and longer trigger pull has been inspired by the safety inherent in the double-action revolver's long, heavy trigger pull. It also eliminates the need for manual safeties, and many striker-fire semiautos don't have them. This satisfied another design goal of law-enforcement and personal-defense needs: making the operating procedure as simple as possible. As any expert will tell you, when firing a handgun under the extreme stress involved in saving your life, simple is good. Glock (Figure 31) is a well known striker-fire handgun manufacturer.

**Figure 31**

## Sidebar: Double-action-only handguns

A DAO handgun may be kept with a round in the chamber. In this state, the gun is considered to be safe. However, a handgun kept in this state, usually for personal protection, still needs to be secured in some other fashion (more on this in *Chapter 7*). As observed in *Chapter 3*, it has long been accepted that the double-action handgun's heavy trigger pull eliminated the need for a separate safety device. Typically, it takes 12 pounds of force to cycle a double-action firing mechanism. While it is theoretically possible for somebody to exert that kind of force unintentionally, it is unheard-of. Also, the hammer or striker of a double-action handgun is at rest; not under spring pressure, waiting to be released.

Taken together, these two facts cause most gun-familiar people to regard the double-action revolver or semiauto as a basically safe gun that needs no additional buttons or levers to prevent accidental firing. Once again, a handgun kept loaded needs to be under the direct supervision of a trained person or secured in some other fashion.

In contrast, the single-action's hammer, when cocked, is waiting to fall. Its short, relatively light trigger pull, typically four pounds or less, raises concerns about unintentional (or negligent) discharges and legal liability.

A person under stress might inadvertently exert the slight trigger pressure needed to fire a cocked single-action gun. Lawsuits alleging that police officers have done just that—unintentionally fired their guns—have resulted in some law-enforcement agencies requiring their officers to carry guns that can be fired only with a longer and heavier trigger pull.

## Review: Firing mode

Let's quickly review the firing mode options for handguns:
- Single-action (SA)—The trigger only releases the hammer. Single-action revolvers must be manually cocked. Single-action semiautos must be manually cocked for the first shot using the thumb or by operating the slide to chamber a round. Every time a single-action semiauto is fired, the slide cycle will cock the hammer automatically.
- Double-action (DA)—A long trigger pull cocks the hammer and then releases it.
- Double-action/single-action (DA/SA)—A semiauto that may

fire the first cartridge double action and subsequent cartridges single action. For revolvers, each round may be fired using either single- or double-action modes.

- Double-action only (DAO) — A DAO semiauto or revolver (typically hammerless) fires all cartridges with a longer, heavier trigger pull.

## Sidebar: Lightweight handguns

Another modern trend, one of the few that might surprise our gun-familiar Rip Van Winkle from the early 1900s, is the lightness of some modern handguns. There is only one reason to make a gun light, and that is to make it less burdensome to carry.

As state after state has passed laws to allow law-abiding citizens to carry guns, so the market for lighter guns has grown.

Many semiautos use composite plastic materials and lighter aluminum or scandium-

**Figure 32**

aluminum alloys in their frames and actions (although slides and barrels are still made of steel), resulting in considerable weight reductions (Figure 32).

Recently, some gun makers have turned to such metals as titanium and aluminum alloys including scandium-aluminum alloys for revolver frames and cylinders (Figure 33). Combined with diminutive size, such guns can be astonishingly light, as little as 12 ounces in some cases.

As with almost all handgun characteristics, trade-offs have consequences. In the case of very light handguns, accuracy and level of recoil are impacted. Lighter guns tend to be harder to shoot.

Although some politicians created a flurry of concern in the 1980s by announcing that "plastic guns" could be brought aboard

**Figure 33**

airliners, the fact is that metal remains a major component in the makeup of any gun, and no gun made anywhere in the world can get past even a simple metal detector.

As we said at the beginning of this chapter, it appears that after centuries of handgun development—at times startlingly innovative development—very little has changed in the past century. The market appears to be satisfied for now.

*And remember - Safety is your responsibility.*

# CHAPTER 2
# Ammunition

We will use the proper words right from the start. A *bullet* is the projectile that comes out of the gun. A *cartridge* is what goes in (Figure 34). They are two different things. The cartridge is composed of a brass, steel or aluminum case, propellant (commonly called gunpowder), and primer. Friction holds the bullet in the case's mouth, or *neck*. If you call a cartridge a bullet, people who are familiar with guns won't say anything rude or discourteous, but they will think you don't understand the basics. Loaded cartridges, also called *rounds*, hold bullets ready for firing. Once a cartridge has been fired, all that remains is the case containing the used primer.

**Figure 34**

## A welcome solution

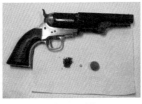

**Figure 35**

Cartridge ammunition is the answer to a problem that confounded arms makers for centuries. Up until the late 1800s, shooters had to load each shot with a laborious process that involved pouring a measured amount of powder down the muzzle of the barrel, next inserting a patch, then topping it off with a lead ball (Figure 35). A ramrod was used to cram the ball and patch down the bore as far as it would go. Finally, they had to prime their weapon. As late as the 1860s, shooters had to place a tiny percussion cap over a nipple at the breech end of the gun. All of this had to be done before cocking the hammer. After all this work, the shooter could fire just one bullet. As you can see, this process is not only time-consuming, it is confusing to a newcomer.

Attempts were made as early as the 1700s to devise all-in-one packages, or "cartridges" as they were being called, to simplify the procedure.

Inventors made a variety of missteps in trying to combine the elements of powder, bullet, and primer. For example, the "pinfire" cartridge of the 1850s placed the primer deep inside the case, where it had to be reached by a long, narrow firing pin that pierced deep inside the cartridge.

By the 1860s, the all-metal rimfire cartridge (Figure 36) was gaining acceptance. It combined bullet, powder, and primer inside a brass case. The rimfire cartridge was the first success in meeting the marketplace demand for the easy loading of a gun.

The final step in the process was the development of the centerfire cartridge, which had the primer in the center of the head (back

**Figure 36**

end) of a cartridge. These were being made in the 1870s, and dominated the industry by the end of the century. Today, rimfire and centerfire are almost the only kinds of cartridges made.

## The components of a cartridge

### Bullets

We'll begin with the bullet, which is what the cartridge is all about. The whole purpose of a gun is to send that small slug downrange at great speed.

The bullet is seated in the case, forced in under pressure so it's lodged securely. Some cases and bullets have a groove, called a cannelure, that runs around the circumference. These are used in the manufacturing process and serve one of several functions, depending on where they are located. They have little to no effect on performance.

Bullets are usually made of lead, although other materials such as steel or copper are used in combination with, or occasionally instead of, lead. Lead is heavy enough to provide some weight to what is, after all, a pretty small package. (Since we'll be mentioning weight in "grains" from time to time, it's worth noting that there are 7,000 grains in a pound.)

Take the 9mm Luger cartridge, for example. It would take about 61 of the standard 115-grain bullets from that cartridge to make up just one pound. About 30 bullets would be needed to make up a pound from the well-known .45 caliber auto cartridge, which typically uses 230-grain bullets. Lead is heavy, bullets are small.

Lead is relatively soft and malleable. When fired, it doesn't batter the inside of the barrel the way that steel would. It conforms nicely to the spiral grooves inside the bore of the barrel.

That's important, because a bullet traveling down the bore is doing two things: it is blocking the expanding gasses behind it from sneaking past and being wasted, and it is being rotated by the bore's spiral grooves. When it emerges, it will be spinning very rapidly.[4]

For example, if the grooves spiral at a rate of one full rotation for every 12 inches, and if the bullet is traveling at 1,000 feet per second, it will be spinning at 60,000 RPM.

That spinning stabilizes the bullet in flight, just as a quarterback spirals a football to stabilize it. (An object sailing through the air that doesn't spin is unstable. Think of hitters in baseball, who dread the knuckleball with its unpredictable flight path. We don't want that.)

Usually, the lead bullet is jacketed (coated) in some metal such as copper alloy, although it does not have to be. It will work either way. Jacketed bullets usually function better in semiautos. Unjacketed lead ammunition is usually less expensive than jacketed, but it may also leave lead smears in the bore that are tedious to remove.

---

[4] The rate of spin is determined by the lands and grooves of the barrel. The tighter (more) the lands and grooves, the faster the spin.

## Bullet shapes

Form always follows function. For general shooting, the typical bullet is copper jacketed and has a rounded nose — in fact, the very kind of nose that comes to mind when we say "bullet nose" (Figure 37).

**Figure 37**

For target shooting, a wadcutter or semi-wadcutter is often used. A wadcutter is cylindrical with a flat nose. A semi-wadcutter resembles a cone with its nose cut off flat (Figure 38). It is also referred to as a truncated cone. The idea behind these bullets is that they cut out a neat circle in the target, which should minimize arguments about whether the bullet did or did not nick a particular area, such as the bullseye. In general, jacketed bullets without cavities in the nose are referred to as "hardball."

**Figure 38**

**Figure 39**

**Figure 40**

Hollowpoints (Figure 39) and soft-points (Figure 40) are hunting, law-enforcement, and self-defense bullets. They are designed to open up, or mushroom, when striking a target (for example, the body of a deer). Police also use hollowpoints to increase the likelihood of incapacitating attackers, and to eliminate over-penetration and ricochets that might injure others.

As in all other areas of life, from tennis rackets to computers to automobiles, manufacturers compete for buyers' dollars. It's the same with bullets. Manufacturers make claims about the effectiveness of different bullet shapes.

Some specialized self-defense bullets are also marketed. For example, one manufacturer encases a load of BB-like pellets in a thinly walled bullet. The idea is that if the round is fired inside a dwelling, any misses

**Figure 41**

will splash harmlessly against a wall rather than penetrating and possibly harming some innocent person on the other side. Broadly speaking, these are called "frangible" bullets. After the September 11, 2001, terrorist attacks, several bullets of this general type were proposed for law enforcement use on airlines.

For a beginning shooter, standard jacketed cartridges will work just fine (Figure 41).

## Case

The container of the cartridge is the case, or casing (Figure 42). It's usually made of brass, which is flexible, malleable, and corrosion-resistant. Other metals, including aluminum, are sometimes used, but brass is inexpensive and does the job very well. (At the range, you'll probably see efforts made to save brass cases. Many shooters reload, and many ranges collect brass that shooters leave behind and sell it to "reloaders.")

**Figure 42**

The bullet end of the case is called the "mouth." The other end is called the "base" or "head." The writing on the head is called the "head-stamp" (more on this shortly).

**Figure 43**

Rimfire cases (Figure 43) are used for the .17 and .22 caliber cartridges in various sizes, such as Short, Long, Long Rifle, and Winchester Magnum Rimfire. The rimfire's primer is inside the projecting rim, hence the name.

Centerfire cases (Figure 44) also get their name from the location of the primer: it's in the center of the base of the case. The primer is in a soft metal cup seated in a small hole, called the primer pocket. Like the rimfire, the centerfire's primer contains an impact-sensitive chemical compound that shoots out sparks, igniting the propellant when the primer is partially crushed by the firing pin.

**Figure 44**

As long as we're looking at the base of the case (which is most commonly referred to as the head rather than the base), you'll notice it has some information inscribed on it. This is called the headstamp. It describes what kind of cartridge it is, including the caliber and manufacturer. In such a cramped space, however, there's only enough room for abbreviations. For example, "W--W 45 COLT" translates to Winchester Western .45 Colt. With .22 Rimfire ammunition, there's only enough room for an abbreviation of the manufacturer's name on the headstamp, so you have to look at the box to find the caliber.

"Gunpowder"

**Figure 45**

Inside the case, you'll find the propellant which, as you know, is a rapidly burning granulated chemical compound (Figure 45). Modern cartridges do not use gunpowder.

True gunpowder, or black powder, is a mixture of sulfur, charcoal and saltpeter. Black powder was used for centuries. In fact, it was the standard propellant used until the late 1800s. As a result, many antique guns still in existence were made to fire black-powder cartridges. That means they are not built to withstand the far higher pressures generated by modern smokeless propellants. Never use modern propellants in an antique gun.

Black powder will detonate if a flame touches it in open air or, of course, inside of a gun. These days, it is used mostly by black-powder shooters who enjoy tradition and making big clouds of smoke. It is unlikely that you will come across this type of propellant.

Modern smokeless powder is far more powerful than black powder. Smokeless powder comes in three shapes: extruded, spherical and flake. All smokeless powders start with a nitrocellulose base (also called "guncotton") and are single-base powders. Add nitroglycerine, and you have a double-based powder that is sometimes called "ballistite" or "Nobel powder" (yes, it was named after the inventor of dynamite and the founder of the Nobel Prize). Add nitroguanidine, and you've got a triple-based powder. Each increase in base level increases the available burn rate and pressure output capability. Ignited in the open, none of these compounds will explode. Rather, they will burn rapidly, generating their own oxygen as they burn. When burned in the confined space of a cartridge case, the heat and pressure (from the oxygen being created) rapidly build up, as does the speed of the reaction feeding on itself and creating ever more pressure.

Smokeless powders used in standard cartridge loads are three times more powerful than their black-powder predecessor and, depending on the burn rate and mixture of base ingredients, can be even more powerful. Cleaner, and more powerful? Is it any surprise that shooters would adopt such an improvement in technology?

## Primer

The primer is the sparkplug of the cartridge. The firing pin strikes the primer, and the resulting chemical reaction generates a small yet sufficient spark. That spark ignites the propellant, which burns extremely quickly and generates a relatively large amount of gas by-product (this is not too dissimilar from what hap-

pens inside a gas engine when the sparkplug ignites the gas fumes inside

**Figure 46**

the engine's cylinder, forcing the piston down). There are three types of primers used in pistol cartridge ammunition. Two are centerfire style primers (Figure 46); the third is the rimfire primer (Figure 47). Today, ammuni-

tion manufacturers use the term "priming systems" to acknowledge that the priming cup and priming compound both play a role in igniting the propellant. In fact, the rimfire priming system was invented as a case

**Figure 47**

and compound system. We are not going to discuss the history of the chemical compounds or the chemistry of current priming compounds (it's more complicated than the propellant description). Just know that when the priming compound is crushed, it delivers enough spark to ignite the propellant.

**Rimfire** ammunition was first made in 1858. Currently, rimfire cartridges dominate the .17 and .22 caliber cartridges in the short, long and magnum varieties. Rimfire cartridges do not use a primer cup. The primer is spun into the rim, which is the fold at the base of the case. These cartridges are not reloadable. People have experimented with rimfire priming in larger caliber ammunition (the .44, .45 and .50 calibers), but creating the rim weakened the already soft and thin case.

**Boxer primer** ammunition (Figure 48) is manufactured for the U.S. market. It comes in two pistol sizes (and, therefore, two different primer compound loads). It is also manufactured in a magnum version for each size of cartridge that uses a larger load of propellant or needs a "hotter" ignition. The unique characteristic of the Boxer priming system is the anvil built into the priming cup. This allows the case to have a single center flash hole. The Boxer

**Figure 48**

primer system is preferred for reloading. It has the reputation of being easier to remove, reconfigure and reload. The Boxer priming system was invented by Edward Boxer, a British ordnance officer.

**Berdan primers** are used throughout the rest of the world. Until NATO standardized its cartridges, Berdan primers were predominant in military rifle ammunition. They have no primer cup anvil. They rely on anvil that is built into the case, with two or three flash holes surrounding it. Berdan primers are not generally considered to be reloadable. They were invented by Hiram Berdan, an American ordnance officer. As reloading becomes more popular worldwide, it is predicted that the Berdan primers will continue to lose popularity.

## Cartridge designations

Handgun cartridges are generally named according to their bullet diameters, but only loosely. The name may also reference the handgun maker for which the cartridge is manufactured. Shooters speak of a ."38" or a "9mm" or a ."22 Long Rifle" cartridge, but it's only a label, and not a scientifically precise one at that.

The numbers are almost never the exact diameter of the bullet, either in millimeters or decimal fractions of an inch—they're just a useful shorthand. The exact diameter of a .38 Special bullet is .357 inch, but it is still referred to as a .38. The number in any cartridge name is usually just an approximation.

So one should ask, "what's in a name?" When it comes to handguns and ammunition, *it is all in the name.*

There are inviolate safety rules when it comes to using ammunition in handguns. We will cover them all within this text, beginning with this one:

*Always, always use the proper ammunition, the precise cartridge specifically designed for the handgun you are shooting.*

The correct ammunition will ensure the proper function of the handgun and the avoidance of what could be a terrible and painful accident.

As indicated above, cartridge manufacturers will usually use a number followed by a word or another number, such as ".44 Special," "9mm Luger," ".45 ACP," ".380 auto," "38 S&W Spec," ".22 Long Rifle," or "9 by 19." Any such named cartridge needs to match the chamber stamp on the frame or barrel of the handgun. It is worth repeating: *always, always use the*

*proper ammunition for the handgun you are shooting.*

Occasionally, a cartridge will have two names. For example, the ".45 Auto" and the ".45 ACP" are the exact same cartridge. ("ACP" stands for Automatic Colt Pistol.) The 9mm Luger is also known as the 9mm Parabellum and the 9 by 19[5].

If in doubt, ask an expert: either a gunsmith or a staff person on the range. And always check the owner's manual. Should the manual not include this information, call the manufacturer. Phone numbers are listed in the back of this book and in your owner's manual.

Incidentally, firearms manufacturing is one of the few areas where metric and English measurements live side-by-side in harmony. For example, nobody seems to have a problem with switching between talking about 9mm and .38 caliber, which are very close to the same diameter, or 7.62 mm and .30 caliber, which are also very close.

As with so many other aspects of handguns, we reach a fork in the road when we come to revolver and semiauto ammunition.

## Revolver ammunition

Most, but not all, revolver cases are "rimmed," which only means that the rim at the head end projects beyond the side of the case; it has a greater diameter than the case (Figure 49). The function of the rim is to hold the cartridge in place inside the revolver's chamber. The cartridge is prevented from sliding forward by its rim (and from sliding back, incidentally, by the breech face). The rare exception to the rule of rimmed cases for revolvers is when a "rimless" case, such as one normally intended for use in a semiauto, is

**Figure 49**

used. In that case, cartridges are usually held in place with either a "half moon" or "full moon" clip, which holds three or six rounds, respectively.

Revolver ammunition often has a cannelure cut into the bullet. Most revolver ammo is made by squeezing the case mouth around the bullet (a procedure called crimping). Crimping secures the bullet in the case.

---

[5] In this case, the 19 represents the case length in millimeters, which is often used as a designator with modern ammunition, especially in the military. But, with .38/40, the second number refers to the weight, in grains, of the black powder that was once used in the cartridge. Firearms enthusiasts being strongly traditional, the designation is kept even though black powder is not normally used anymore.

## Semiauto ammunition

Most semiauto cases are called "rimless." Yes, the case still has a rim, but it typically doesn't project beyond the body of the case (Figure 50). Generally, the base rim is the same diameter as the case. The rimless design allows cartridges to slide alongside each other easily, so when the cartridge is pushed from the magazine on its way to the chamber, there is nothing to hinder its progress.

**Figure 50**

Semiauto cases have a deep extractor groove forward of the rim to give the extractor claw room to engage the cartridge. (In ordinary operation, as the cartridge enters the chamber, its head slides up the breech face, and the rim slips under the extractor claw.) Manufacturers have found that semiauto cartridges with a very tightly seated bullet and a taper crimp tend to function best. You can't roll crimp semiauto cases (such as 9mm and 45 auto) because the case mouth has to "seat" on a thin ledge at the front of the chamber.

## Selecting ammunition

As stated earlier (and it's worth repeating), *it is vital to use the correct ammunition; using the wrong ammunition is dangerous, even if it seems to fit.*

Almost every gun is clearly marked with the ammunition to be used. The information is typically stamped or printed on the barrel, slide, or frame, and can appear on either side. With revolvers, it's often printed on the right side of the barrel. With semiautos, it may be printed along

**Figure 51**

the slide or on the barrel chamber, where it can be read through the ejection port. On rare occasions, usually with very old guns, there will be no cartridge identification. Check your owner's manual, of course, and ask an expert before firing any ammunition in an unmarked gun. Even call the manufacturer!

Ammunition is also clearly marked on the box it came in (Figure 51), as well as on the headstamp (Figure 52). (An exception is military ammunition, which may include only the date of manufacture and the name of the arsenal.) When in doubt, always check with an expert. *And don't put your ammunition in the wrong box.*

**Figure 52**

Manufacturers sometimes make efforts to prevent chambering incorrect rounds. For example, when the .357 Magnum cartridge was brought out in 1935 as a high-powered hunting round, Smith & Wesson was concerned that shooters might try to fire the cartridges in revolvers chambered for the significantly less powerful .38 Special. Because .38 Special revolvers might not withstand the dramatically increased chamber pressures of the .357, the new cartridge was deliberately made approximately 1/10th of an inch longer so it would not chamber in the .38 Special (Figure 53). However, the .38 Special cartridge will chamber and fire in a .357 handgun without any danger. A chart showing what ammunition can be fired in what gun is provided at the end of this chapter on page 48.

**Figure 53**

There are so many cartridges and so many guns out there, that it is just not possible for every gun to be made incapable of firing the wrong ammunition. So it's up to you to confirm that you are using the right ammunition for your gun. The consequences of using the wrong ammunition can be nasty. Put it this way: The fact that cartridge A seems to fit easily in chamber B does not mean it's okay to pull the trigger. To repeat: Consult the owner's manual and the chart on page 48.

## Checking it out

Let's take a look at a typical box of handgun ammunition, in this case, a white box with the name "Winchester" printed on it in red, plus the warning, in English and French, "Keep out of reach of children."

Here's what it says on the end flaps:

### 9mm LUGER

### 115 GR. FULL METAL JACKET

### TARGET/RANGE

This tells us quite a bit. The word "Luger" after "9mm" ensures that the ammunition is for any pistol that chambers that particular 9mm round; not just the famous Luger semiautomatic, but any pistol chambered for 9mm. There are probably more centerfire pistols that fire this round than any other. (In 2001, about 33 percent of all semiautos made in the U.S. were 9mm, with the next largest category, .40 caliber and larger semiautos, at about 19 percent.)

But there are other kinds of 9mm, and the vast majority of them are *not* interchangeable. We repeat: *Never put a cartridge into a gun chambered for something else unless it is included in the table on page 48.*

Returning to the box now, "115 GR." tells us the weight of the bullet. As we said before, there are 7,000 grains in a pound. This is a typical bullet weight for the 9mm Luger, although other weights are available.

Now, although "FULL METAL JACKET" has a faintly ominous air — it was used as a menacing movie title — it really means that the lead bullet is encased in a copper jacket. As noted earlier, copper adds slightly to the price but is a lot easier to clean up.

The presence of a full metal jacket does not make the bullet more deadly. On the contrary, plain lead bullets tend to expand more than full metal jacketed ones.

The "TARGET/RANGE" information tells us, even before we open the box, that the cartridges have round-nose bullets suitable for general use, including target shooting and "plinking."[6]

The headstamp on the cartridges read "WIN 9mm LUGER." The WIN means Winchester. Because the manufacturer is a big, respected name, we expect that significant quality control went into its production, and that it is safe to use in any gun chambered for the 9mm Luger.

## Increased-pressure ammunition

Some self-defense ammunition is made with more propellant (Figure 54), and is usually sold as "+P" (pronounced "plus P") or "+P+" ("plus P plus"). The first has greater chamber pressure than a standard cartridge; the second has even more.

According to the Remington and Federal law-enforcement ammunition catalogs, standard muzzle velocity for the 9mm Luger 115 grain standard is 1,160 feet per second (fps).

**Figure 54**

The +P cartridge is 1,250 fps, and +P+ is 1,300 fps. Factory-made cartridges that are +P or +P+ always have that information stamped on the case head. Normally, +P+ is marketed only to law enforcement, although it is perfectly legal for civilians to possess and use.

---

[6] "Plinking" is colloquial term for target shooting in general. It gets its name from the sound a bullet makes when it hits a metal plate.

Many handgun manufacturers do not authorize the use of increased-pressure ammunition in their guns. Some do. You should always check the owner's manual for your gun. Avoid using increased-pressure ammunition if it is not specifically authorized.

Because it is vital to match the cartridge to the gun exactly, use the owner's manual and always match the headstamp, cartridge box, and information stamped on the gun itself. All manufacturers will provide a free owner's manual should you need one, and owners' manuals almost always include a section on ammunition selection. If you can't find the information in the manual, call the manufacturer at the number listed in the back of this book.

## "Stopping power"

The point of these increased-pressure rounds is to make the bullet travel faster. Powerful modern handgun ammunition was first developed in the 1930s in response to hunters who wanted to be able to go into the field while carrying a gun in a holster. The first was the .357 Magnum, which was used to take animals, including deer. The .357 was basically a stepped-up .38 Special that moved the bullet a *lot* faster.

The total force of any moving object is calculated by multiplying its weight by its speed. One way to increase force is simply to increase the speed. Adding propellant to increase speed is a surprisingly effective way to increase the force of a bullet without having to make any other changes: same case, same bullet, same primer and, if the manufacturer allows it, same gun.

Increasing speed boosts energy dramatically. Energy delivered to the target is one factor contributing to what is known as *stopping power*. The physics formula is complicated, but what it comes down to is that the two factors, weight and speed, are multiplied and not just added together. If you double the speed of a bullet, you don't double its energy — you quadruple it. This is because energy is proportional to the square of the speed.

### Stopping power from space

To get an idea of what speed can do for a moving object, let's look to aviation. Bill Sweetman, an expert on aeronautics, once speculated about the effects of a 200-pound slug of steel dropped from very high altitude at an extremely high speed, such as Mach 15, or roughly 10,300 miles per hour. "It would lift the battleship Kirov out of the water," he said.

It would also have to be protected from burning up in the atmosphere at that speed, and it would have to be designed so it didn't just pass right through the Kirov, leaving a smoking hole. It would instead have to open up and expend all its energy inside the battleship. Still, that's pretty impressive for a mere 200 pounds of inert metal, and it shows what just adding speed can do for a given amount of weight.

## Back to Earth

Returning to guns, here's what happens using a standard 9mm Luger cartridge with a typical 115-grain bullet fired from a Glock Model 17. The typical speed (muzzle velocity) is about 1,160 feet per second, which is slightly over the speed of sound (sound averages about 1,100 feet per second, depending on temperature).

That's 344 foot-pounds of energy (which means the energy needed to move a 344-pound object one foot, or a one-pound object 344 feet).

If the speed is increased by adding more propellant to achieve 1,400 feet per second, the result is 501 foot-pounds of energy. A 20% increase in speed nets a 46% increase in energy.

For comparison, the .45 ACP round, at 230 grains and moving at 900 feet per second, develops 414 foot-pounds of energy. That's below the pumped-up Luger round. In other words, because of increased speed, the Luger round, which is normally considered far less effective than the .45 Auto because it is only half the weight, acquires greater energy than its big brother.

We thus open up a long-standing controversy among gun enthusiasts. Some argue that, for stopping power, sheer weight and caliber counts for more, no matter what the speed. The opposition argues that the only thing that matters is energy, and increasing speed will have the same effect. We take no side in this controversy; we're just mentioning it.

## Sidebar: Handloaded ammunition

Some shooters handload their own ammunition, using either all new components or recycled cases (this is known as reloaded ammunition). Occasionally, small entrepreneurs offer handloads or reloads for sale at gun shows and elsewhere. There may be nothing wrong with this ammunition—in some cases, it may have been made to very high standards—but if you didn't assemble it yourself, you don't know what you are getting.

We advocate sticking to major manufacturers such as Federal, CCI,

Winchester, Remington, and others with well-established reputations.

## Sidebar: Calculating bullet energy

Square the velocity (in feet per second) and divide it by 64.32 (which is twice the acceleration of gravity). Divide this total by 7000 (the number of grains in a pound) and, finally, multiply this by the bullet weight in grains. That will give you the energy in foot-pounds.

So a .45 cal. 230-grain bullet at 900 fps will yield 414 foot-pounds. (900 x 900 = 810000, divided by 64.32 = 12593.283, divided by 7000 = 1.7990404 x 230 = 413.77929 [414 rounded off] foot-pounds.)

Notice that energy is proportional to the square of the velocity. With equal bullet weights, doubling the velocity produces four times the energy. Tripling the velocity produces nine times the energy. Quadruple it and you get 16 times the energy. This is why rifles produce significantly higher energy levels than handguns.

For example, the .25 cal. Colt semiauto propels its 50-grain bullet at about 800 fps, producing 71 foot-pounds. But an AR-15 rifle, also with a 50-grain bullet, but moving at 3200 fps, produces 1137 foot-pounds, or 16 times the energy.

Now, consider a 3500-pound automobile traveling at 60 mph (88 fps). 88 x 88 divided by 64.32 x 3500 = 421,393 foot-pounds! This might explain why it is far worse to be hit by a car than it is to be shot. So, are cars more dangerous than guns? Yes, they are.

## Sidebar: Acceptable ammunition substitutions

Use this guide for substituting one type of ammunition for another.
Assume that if a cartridge is not listed in the right-hand column as a safe
alternative, it is not safe to use in any gun chambered for the round in
the left-hand column.

| Nominal chambering | Safe alternative |
|---|---|
| .22 Long | .22 Short |
| .22 Long Rifle | .22 Long, .22 Short |
| .22 Win. Mag. Rimfire | .22 Win. Rimfire |
| .32 S&W Long | .32 S&W |
| .32 S&W Long | .32 S&W |
| .32 H&R Mag. | .32 S&W, .32 S&W Long |
| .32 Long Colt | .32 Short Colt |
| .38 Long Colt | .38 Short Colt |
| .38 Special | .38 Long Colt, .38 Short Colt |
| .357 Mag. | .38 Special, .38 Long Colt, and .38 Short Colt |
| .357 Max. | .357 Mag., .38 Special, .38 Long Colt, and .38 Short Colt |
| .38 Super | .38 ACP |
| .41 Long Colt | .41 Short Colt |
| .44 Magnum | .44 Special, .44 Russian |
| .45 Colt | .45 S&W |
| .455 Webley | .450 Short |
| **Note**: Table from American Rifleman magazine. | |

*And remember - Safety is your responsibility.*

# CHAPTER 3
# Gun Safety and Handling

Gun handling and gun safety cannot be separated. To handle a gun is to take one of two opposite directions from the very moment you pick it up: safe or unsafe.

When you pick up a handgun, you immediately discover just how easy it is to rest your finger on the trigger. The gun is made so that your forefinger falls naturally on the trigger and curls around it comfortably. It would be irksome to shoot if it were not made that way.

It takes practice to learn to pick up a gun and rest your forefinger on the trigger guard or, better yet, along the frame above the trigger guard (Figure 55). But that is just what you should do, from the first time you pick up a gun, and for the rest of your life.

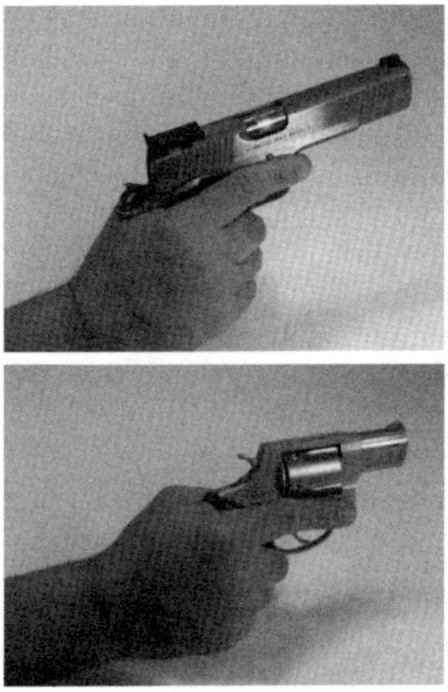

**Figure 55**

Keeping your finger outside the trigger guard does two things, both of them good. First, it prevents you from unconsciously resting your finger on the trigger. Resting your finger there has all too often resulted in tragedy. A person may be inadvertently startled or find himself suddenly off balance and reflexively squeezing the trigger.

Second, it shows those around you that your finger is not on the trigger. Yes, it is possible to have your forefinger inside the trigger guard but not touching the trigger, as bad of form as that is! However, showing others that your finger is not on the trigger is important. It communicates safety and respect.

When you pick up any gun, it will naturally point in some direction. You can let it point toward yourself, your child, your friend, the piano, or the window beyond which your neighbor is raking his lawn. Or, you can point it in a safe direction, such as at the ground, the sky, the attic or the basement if you are sure no one is in the way. The gun moves *at your command*, not on its own.

It's your choice.

You have to choose, and continue to choose, as long as you are holding the gun. If you move, the gun must point to another safe direction. It takes a conscious effort on your part.

Safe and unsafe are the only options you have when you handle a gun. There is no third option; it's one or the other, right from the beginning.

So, the two cardinal rules for handling a handgun, or any gun, are:

1. *Point it in a safe direction.*
2. *Always keep your finger outside the trigger guard.*

Good news: That's about all you have to know to handle a handgun safely. Even if you were to pick up some exotic sidearm made in Belgium, with levers and switches and laser sights, it wouldn't matter. As long as your finger stays outside the trigger guard and the gun is pointed in a safe direction, it will not inadvertently fire, nor can you accidentally do any harm.

Let's get a little more specific and, in this case, repetitious. "Outside the trigger guard" means on the side of the frame, *above* the trigger guard. That way, others can see the trigger and that your finger is not on it. It is hard to overstate the importance of this rule, but believe me, we are going to do our best to do just that! That is how important keeping your finger outside the trigger guard is.

"Pointed in a safe direction" means—well, what's a safe direction at the moment? If you're on the top floor of a building, pointed up would probably be safe. If you're outdoors, down is usually safe. But don't assume that sideways is safe just because there's nobody standing right there. If the gun is pointed toward a sheetrock wall, and there's a person on the other side, then that's not a safe direction. "Safe direction" means whatever direction fits this description: *If the gun were to fire at this moment, nobody will be harmed.* Maintaining a safe direction must become a sixth sense, cultivated by a constant assessment of your surroundings and the relationship the firearm has to those surroundings. Nurturing this awareness has a wonderful side benefit. Even when you are not handling a gun, you will become pleasantly more aware of your surroundings and find yourself noticing the little things in life you might otherwise miss.

If you make these two rules a conscious part of handling any gun, if you incorporate them into your very being and never violate them, whenever you reach for a handgun or any other gun, you will be safe. In time, these rules will become unconscious habits, and you will be as close as possible to never accidentally shooting something or someone.

## Another safety rule

**"Always treat every gun as if it is loaded"** is a good rule, but it is subject to interpretation. Like "drive safely" or "eat right," it lacks specifics.

For example, some people who have owned guns for a long time and should know better will sometimes allow the muzzles of their unloaded guns to wander around and even (accidentally) point at other people for just a moment. They know that the gun is unloaded, yet they are breaking the "point it in a safe direction" rule. They feel that, because the gun is unloaded, it can be treated differently. Well, it can't.

The "treat every gun as if it is loaded" rule applies to every gun— even the gun you left on the workbench just an hour ago after cleaning it, and nobody else has been near it.

This rule also applies to any gun you are dry-firing (deliberately pulling the trigger and allowing the hammer to fall on an empty chamber). You can't assume that the gun will not fire because you think it's not loaded. Perform the clearing procedure, described next, to ensure that it is not loaded before each and every dry-fire session. When dry-firing a handgun, you must also point it in a safe direction. You are, after all, about to break one of the cardinal rules and insert your finger inside the trigger guard. You are even going to pull the trigger. So making sure the handgun is unloaded and pointed in a safe direction before pulling the trigger is critical. *Do it every time!*

As we will see below, guns have a way of not being empty when people think they are. "Innocent until proven guilty" is a longstanding judicial axiom. "Loaded until proven unloaded" is the axiom for guns. Assume every gun is loaded until proven otherwise.

And even then:

1.  *Point it in a safe direction.*
2.  *Always keep your finger outside the trigger guard.*

## Clearing procedure

Every time we pick up a gun, we go through a clearing procedure to ensure it is not loaded. A clearing procedure can also be used as part of a pre-firing check if you are about to shoot a firearm you have not previously checked. It is also vital to perform a clearing procedure when you have finished firing the gun, be it at the range, hunting, or after informal target practice. The procedure is the same whether you pick up the firearm to clean it, hand it to another person, or just look it over.

The clearing procedure performs three important functions: it (1) unloads the gun, (2) verifies that the gun is unloaded, and (3) prepares the gun for the next step — cleaning, handing to another person, or putting away. You may easily find yourself going through this procedure a dozen times during one session at the range.

As you might guess, these procedures were developed over a very long time and are based on common sense. The method differs for revolvers and semiautos. If the method described here varies from your owner's manual, follow what's in the owner's manual.

## Double-action revolver

Keeping the gun pointed in a safe direction and your finger outside the trigger guard, press the cylinder latch and swing the cylinder out of the frame (Figure 56). Remove any cartridges from the chambers with the ejector rod. Pushing in the ejector rod insures that all cartridges are out of the cylinder (Figure 57). Make that a habit. Then, actually look into each chamber and the barrel.

**Figure 56**

It's now okay to proceed with cleaning or whatever else you were going to do.

To hand a revolver to another person, leave the cylinder swung out of the frame and hand it over with your thumb through the cylinder opening and the barrel pointed down (Figure 58). Don't allow the gun to point at anybody, including

**Figure 57**

**Figure 58**

yourself. This way, you guarantee that the action is open throughout the pass. The recipient grasps the gun at the grip, holding the cylinder swung out, and keeps the muzzle pointed in a safe direction.

## Single-action revolver

For single-action revolvers, the cylinder can't be swung out, so the method is to point the muzzle in a safe direction and open the loading gate. Some guns' cylinders can be rotated freely just by having the gate open; others require that the hammer be drawn back to the loading notch position (this is about a one-half to three-quarter cocked position, depending on the model). In any case, if the muzzle is pointing upward, unfired cartridges should fall out as pass the loading gate. However, get

**Figure 59**

in the habit of using the ejector rod for each chamber—every time (Figure 59).

It is then okay to hand the gun to someone while it is pointed in a safe direction.

## Semiauto

Pointing the gun in a safe direction and keeping your finger outside the trigger guard, press the magazine release to remove the magazine (Figure 60). *Always remove the magazine first!* Then, briskly pull the slide back and let it slam forward three times. Pull the slide back again and lock it open if possible (Figure 61). Visually examine the inside of the gun: chamber, breech area, and magazine well. You can also perform a physical check by inserting the tip of your little finger into the chamber, breech area, and magazine well to ensure there are no cartridges present. (Note that if your finger disengages the slide stop from the inside, the slide can slam forward on your finger. This is an experience you really don't want to have, so be careful.) If the slide cannot be locked open, hold it open and perform a complete visual inspection to ensure that the handgun is completely "clear" of cartridges.

**Figure 60**

**Figure 61**

Many semi-autos have an external slide lock. In some, the safety or a takedown lever may lock the slide open. A good number of semiautos have only an internal slide lock. To lock these slides open, you must insert an *empty* magazine and then draw the slide back fully. As noted above, some semiautos have no slide lock at all and must be held open for inspection. In any case, *always* make sure that the chamber, breech area, and magazine well are empty. *Take note of the sequence.* The gun is first emptied of cartridges, and then examined. Also note what happens if the sequence gets messed up, say, by operating the slide and *then* removing a loaded magazine. That's a loaded gun with a round in the chamber. *Don't do that.*

**Figure 62**

To hand a semiauto to another person, keep the gun pointed in a safe direction, perform the clearing procedure, and show the empty breech area to the recipient. Grasp the slide and point the butt of the grip (the empty magazine well) at the recipient. The recipient grasps the grip, making sure the muzzle is pointed in a safe direction (Figure 62). The order of events is important: the gun is emptied of cartridges, then shown to be empty, and then safely handed over.

## One bad idea

One really bad handing-over technique is to hand the gun to a person simply by grasping it by the barrel and extending the grip towards the other person, with the barrel pointing back at you. It may be polite, but it is also stupid and dangerous.

This dangerous act almost certainly comes from movies and TV, because it's hard to imagine our ancestors being foolish enough to handle guns in this way. The act is fairly common on the screen, when the defeated ones (cops, robbers, cattle rustlers, whomever), having lost the encounter, are told "Okay, boys, hand 'em over."

Do not hand a gun over that way. Doing so violates the point-in-safe-direction rule (it's pointed at *you*). Not only that, it presents the recipient with a chance to stick his or her finger inside the trigger guard.

## One good idea

Any time you hand a gun over, it's a good idea for the giver to say, "You've got it," and the recipient to say, "I've got it."

## An exception to handing it over empty

On occasion, and under certain circumstances, such as at a shooting station at the range, you might hand a loaded gun to a person. Do so

ONLY if the person is clearly informed of its loaded state. When handing the gun over, keep it pointed downrange and be sure that all fingers are kept off the trigger.

## Practical applications

Having described in broad terms the best way (in many experts' eyes, the only way) to hand a gun to another person, let's examine some hypothetical examples.

Your friend **Bob** says he just bought a Smith & Wesson model 686 revolver in .357 magnum. He opens the case and grasps the gun by the grip, but with his forefinger resting on the frame above the trigger guard.

So far, privately, you're giving Bob an "A."

He then hands it to you without opening the cylinder and showing you the empty chambers, and he also negligently lets the muzzle swing past your body.

He has just violated one basic rule by pointing the gun at somebody, and he hasn't observed the "showing-it-empty" protocol.

Privately, you revise his grade to "F." But what are you going to do about it? In real life, most of us are not comfortable openly correcting others, so we usually just don't say anything. What you can do is engage in actions that speak for themselves. Immediately upon receiving the firearm, open the cylinder, check the chambers and then holster or otherwise safely position the gun. That should cause Bob to recognize his error and apologize. If he doesn't, it seems you'd be well advised to avoid Bob when he's anywhere near a gun.

Then there's **Cathy**. She hands you her Colt 1911 .45 Auto while keeping her finger outside the trigger guard and without pointing it at you or anybody else. You have no idea whether it's loaded. Is she a poor gun handler?

We'd give Cathy a C. She should have done the clearing procedure described above, to show you the gun was empty before handing it to you. It's now up to you to check the gun yourself. Cathy didn't endanger you, but she didn't play by all the rules.

Finally, there's **Mark.** He brings his new Ruger .22 semiauto in a soft, zippered pistol rug over to your house to show you. As he slips it out of its rug, he is scrupulous about where he points it. He keeps his finger outside the trigger guard, performs the clearing procedure, locks the slide back, and shows you the chamber and magazine well are empty before handing the gun to you. Up to this point, Mark gets an A.

But, after the pistol is back inside its gun rug, he puts it down on the couch next to him with the muzzle end of the rug pointing at you. Is that unsafe?

Well, there's some debate about that. Guns that are properly stored (in safes, for example) have to be pointing in *some* direction. Sooner or later, a person will pass in front of the muzzle. Broadly speaking, a gun that is not loaded (are you sure it's not loaded?), is not being handled, and is in a closed container of some sort is not considered to be endangering anybody.

## What happens when things go bad?

**Larry** is a somewhat forgetful fellow who would really profit from making the clearing procedure a part of his life. He does not always remove the magazine from his Glock 9mm pistol and look through the ejection port to confirm that the chamber, breech, and magazine well are empty. He bases his actions on whether he thinks the gun is unloaded rather than on visually confirming that it is. Most of the time, he's right about the gun's condition.

One day in his workshop, Larry picks up his Glock and drops the magazine out of its well. Assuming he has unloaded the gun, he then takes careful aim at a cordless drill on the workbench and carefully squeezes the trigger for a practice dry-fire.

The gun fires and recoils in his hand, the $180 drill tumbles end-over-end across the workbench shedding parts, and his ears are filled with a high-pitched ringing.

His alarmed wife rushes downstairs to see what happened. He announces, "The gun went off."

For Larry, we need a grade well below an F. Larry is a danger to himself and others. (And we can't resist adding that Larry is just the kind of guy who will stand there with the gun in his hand, inadvertently pointing at his wife, his finger resting on the trigger, while he's talking.)

By the way, "the gun went off" as an excuse is wholly inaccurate. Larry fired the gun, pure and simple. Modern handguns *do not* go off by themselves: not while cleaning them, not while storing them, and not when they are dropped. Modern handguns go off only when the trigger is pulled.

## Putting it all together

Let's take one more theoretical person, **Sam**, who gets it right all the way through.

Sam was cleaning his new Smith & Wesson Model 4013TSW .40 caliber semiauto when his friend Tom stopped by to see the new gun.

Sam greets Tom at the door and shows him to the basement workbench, where he has just finished cleaning the gun after firing it at the range. The pistol sits there, reassembled. Even though he knows that it's empty, Tom still regards the gun as loaded until proven unloaded.

He performs a clearing procedure. Keeping the gun pointed in a safe direction and his finger outside the trigger guard, Sam removes the magazine. Then, he briskly pulls the slide back and lets it slam forward three times. He then locks the slide back, visually and physically inspects the chamber, breech area and magazine well, shows the empty breech to Tom and, finally, hands it to him grip first, with the muzzle pointed down.

A-plus.

Now let's hope Tom also treats the gun safely. If everybody treated guns the way Sam does, there would never be another negligent discharge, and no gun would ever be said to "go off."

## Handling

Let's acknowledge a reality: most people will learn basic gun handling from a family member or a knowledgeable friend.

Let's acknowledge another reality: Your uncle Jim, who's been around guns all his life, may actually be an expert, or he may not be as knowledgeable as he claims. Actual experts are the sources you should turn to. If you have any doubts about uncle Jim's knowledge and reliability, turn to a local gun range, an NRA club, a certified instructor (such as an AACFI instructor), or a gun store to provide names of reliable people.

For the technical workings of the gun, turn to the manufacturer's owner's manual. More detailed manuals are sold at gun stores, gun shows, and on the Internet. And don't forget your local library. Also, develop a relationship with a local gunsmith.

Actual gun handling is fairly simple, although not quite as simple as Hollywood has made it out to be.

The following does not replace your owner's manual, nor does it take the place of expert instruction. It is a guide to what you can expect to learn from knowledgeable people. We hope it will shorten the learning time for you. Responsible gun handling is like learning to drive. You can watch all the instructional movies and read all the literature, but until you are properly coached, you will never master the principles of handling either a gun or a car.

Loaded revolvers and semiautos are handled somewhat differently.

## Handling revolvers

Today, the most common type of revolver is the double-action. Your first step in handling one is to ensure that it is unloaded, then check it to be sure it will function properly.

To ensure that it is unloaded, while keeping it pointed in a safe direction and with your finger outside the trigger guard, perform the clearing procedure as described on page 52.

To ensure proper function, start by checking the bore (the inside of the barrel). You want to make sure there are no obstructions. Significant obstructions in the bore could cause the gun to blow up when fired. This is highly unlikely, but possible. The simplest way is just to look, but that of course means you'll be pointing the gun in a very unsafe direction — at yourself. So, *you must have the cylinder open to check.* (You would have to anyway, just to allow enough light in to look down the bore.)

**Figure 63**

Manipulating the gun in such a way as to look down the barrel may violate the rules at some ranges about always keeping the gun pointed downrange. In this case, use a cleaning rod with the proper size of brush attached. No rod? Run something like a wooden pencil down the bore (Figure 63). Or, you can shine a small flashlight down the bore and look for a clear round spot on the recoil shield or the back of a business card (Figure 64). (You'll have to hold the flashlight about a foot in front of the muzzle to get the bright circle in sharp focus.) You just want to confirm that the bore is free of debris. A smearing of lead or a few granules of powder are acceptable.

To continue checking function, close the cylinder and cock the gun by pulling the

**Figure 64**

hammer back with your thumb until it clicks into the fully cocked position. Point the gun in a safe direction (downrange), then pull the trigger to "dry-fire" it (allow the hammer to fall on an empty chamber) a couple of times. You are looking for normal, smooth functioning. The cylinder will revolve, and the hammer will rise and then fall, all very smoothly. Avoid excessive dry-firing, which can slowly damage some revolvers.[7] If the cylinder needs to be manually rotated into place after the hammer is cocked or after dry firing, the gun is defective and must not be fired.

Hold the gun sideways up to a bright light and look through the gap at the back of the cylinder to confirm that when the trigger is released, the firing pin is retracted behind the recoil shield. Check the gap at the front of the cylinder where it lines up with the barrel. Generally, the cylinder-barrel gap should be a little thicker than a standard piece of copy paper but thinner than a business card.

### Cowboy-style single-action

With these, the cylinder doesn't swing out, but you can still check the cylinder for snugness when the hammer is cocked and during dry-firing. The owner's manual will tell you how to remove the base pin so the cylinder can be lifted out entirely. Then, you can either run a pencil down the bore or use the flashlight method described earlier.

### Loading the revolver

**Figure 65**

Make absolutely certain you are using the correct ammunition. This information is almost always printed on the right side of the gun, usually on the barrel (Figure 65); for example, ".357 MAGNUM," ".22 CAL LONG RIFLE," ".44 SPECIAL." In each case, the information tells you exactly what cartridge must be used in the gun. In *Chapter 2*, we go into the subject in detail. For now, it is enough to say that you should match the gun with the information on the ammunition box (Figure 66). The headstamp on the back of the cartridge case should also agree

**Figure 66**

---

[7] Any time you are dry-firing a lot, use "snap-caps," which are dummy rounds made specifically for dry-firing.

(Figure 67). If in doubt, see the owner's manual.

*In certain cases,* it is safe to use ammunition other than that specified on the side of the gun. For example, .38 Special cartridges can be fired in a gun chambered for the .357 Magnum. (In *Chapter 2,* you will find a table that lists the ammunition that can be safely fired from certain guns.) If you don't know for a fact that other ammunition can be used, do not use it. If you are in doubt, ask a pro. Using the wrong ammunition is very dangerous.

Figure 67

To load a revolver, swing out the cylinder of a double-action, or open the loading gate on the right side of a cowboy-style single-action, then drop the cartridges into each individual chamber (Figure 68).

Figure 68

**Note**: If any cartridge doesn't slide easily into place, examine it for defects. If it still gives trouble, stop loading the gun. Either the cartridge is defective, it's the wrong ammunition, or something about the gun is defective. The gun also could be very dirty! Unload the gun and take both it and the ammunition to a gunsmith.

Ordinarily, the cartridges will slide in easily, and the cylinder or the loading gate will then close easily.

## The revolver is ready to fire

The typical double-action can be fired in two ways. One is to draw the trigger back through its long, heavy pull (Figure 69). This single movement rotates the cylinder, cocks the hammer and, at the end of the pull, releases the sear so the hammer falls and fires the cartridge. This method is referred to as "double-action firing."

Figure 69

The other method, and the only one available with a single-action

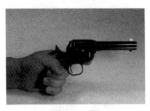

revolver, is to first manually cock the hammer, and then pull the trigger (Figure 70). This, naturally, is called "single-action firing." It is usually chosen when the shooter is trying to get off a very accurate shot.

Most people have trouble holding the gun steady during the long, heavy double-action trigger pull. Most find the very short, light single-action pull much friendlier when shooting for accuracy. A typical double-action pull takes 12 to 15 pounds of force (imagine lifting a bowling ball with your index finger). A single-action pull, on the other hand, takes about four to six.

**Figure 70**

## Stoppages, jams, and failures to fire

Jams are nearly unheard-of with revolvers (unlike semiautos). Few people will ever encounter one. That said, if the gun balks in any way (the gun, not an ammunition failure), immediately open the cylinder and remove all cartridges. If the cylinder can't be opened (this is incredibly rare, but it can happen), block the hammer if it is cocked, case the gun, and take it to a gunsmith. Let the gunsmith know there are cartridges in the gun.

If the cylinder rotates correctly when no ammunition is inserted, but slows or stops when rounds are in the chamber, there are several possibilities.

Incorrect seating of the primer may cause it to drag on the recoil shield, hindering cylinder rotation. Or, the gap between the recoil shield and the headstamp is slightly less than the thickness of the business card. Replace the ammunition.

On some guns, repeated dry firing can cause the metal around the firing-pin hole in the recoil shield to rise up like a tiny volcano and drag against case heads as the cylinder rotates. A gunsmith can deal with this problem easily. If this happens to your gun, dry-fire only with "snap caps" in the gun. Snap caps are dummy cartridges with spring-loaded primers that absorb the energy from the firing pin. They are sold at most gun stores.

Stoppages can also be caused when the lockwork within the gun jams. This malfunction is beyond the capabilities of most gun owners and should be corrected by a gunsmith.

Occasionally, on revolvers that are not cleaned thoroughly, powder residue will build up in the upper corner of the frame opening, just above the barrel-cylinder gap. The same can happen under the ejector star. Check for this problem if the cylinder is reluctant to rotate (whether loaded or unloaded), or if the cylinder is reluctant to swing out or back in. The powder residue can be removed with solvent and a stiff bristle brush. See *Chapter 6*.

When shooting, if at any time you hear or feel *anything* unusual (for example, if any round looks, feels, or sounds unlike other shots), *stop shooting immediately!* Perform a clearing procedure and examine the gun and ammunition.

## Malfunctions—Stop shooting immediately

An unusually mild-sounding report (noise from firing) is potentially very dangerous. The bullet may have traveled partway down the bore and stopped. This is known as a *squib-load*, and is generally caused by a cartridge with an improper amount of propellant. If another round is fired, that obstruction can cause the barrel to blow apart. Unload the cylinder and check the bore to be sure there is no obstruction.

Should the revolver function properly and the cartridge fail to fire, remain in your firing position and keep the firearm pointed downrange for one minute. Although rare, you may be experiencing a *hang-fire*—a delayed firing due to a defective primer. The odds against a hang-fire firing after 60 seconds are astronomical, so it's probably safe to extract the round and ask the range officers what to do with the dud.

In general, if the gun does not function smoothly in any way, unload it and take it to a gunsmith.

## Unloading a revolver after firing

To unload a double-action revolver, swing the cylinder out and firmly push the ejector rod (Figure 71). This will eject all the cartridges from the gun onto the ground or into a suitable container.

After rounds have been fired, the spent cases may have expanded so much that they require an extra push, which is why the gun is

**Figure 71**

equipped with an ejector. It's actuated by the rod under the barrel, which swings out with the cylinder. Different ammunition will behave differently in different guns. Some spent cases will fall out easily; others will require a little shove.

To unload a cowboy-style single-action firearm (Figure 72), you must open the loading gate, and may have to partially cock the hammer to the unloading notch (this allows the cylinder to rotate freely). Hold the gun so the muzzle is pointed upward and rotate the cylinder. Use the ejector rod to remove each spent case from the chamber.

**Figure 72**

## Handling semiautos

Semiautos come in a variety of styles and types. Please check your owner's manual for specifics. Let's look at a typical pistol, the Colt Model 1911 .45 Auto, upon which most semiautos are based.

Perform the clearing procedure described above.

Confirm that the bore is free of debris. If you are at the range, and the rules prohibit manipulating the gun in such a way that you can look down the bore, you can run a pencil down it (Figure 73) or shine a flashlight down it and look for a clean circle on the bolt face.

You can also field-strip[8] the gun to check it. As with a revolver, a smear of lead and a few granules of powder are acceptable.

**Figure 73**

Verifying the proper functioning of a semiauto is a multi-step process. Check for normal slide operation by removing the magazine and operating the slide.

Ensure normal trigger operation by dry-firing several times. Next, check to be sure the safety and/or de-cocking mechanism (if the gun is so equipped), and magazine release function properly.

Finally, verify the function of the disconnector by performing two checks.

The first check is to dry fire the gun and, while holding the trigger back, manually operate the slide. Now, release the trigger fully and dry-fire a second time to verify trigger reset.

---

[8] Field-stripping refers to a basic, minimal disassembly for routine maintenance and cleaning. It's described in your owner's manual. We strongly urge every semiauto owner to become so familiar with his or her gun that field-stripping is a quick and easy procedure.

The second check requires that you pull the slide slightly out of battery (slightly to the rear, approximately 1/4 of an inch) and pull the trigger (Figure 74). Pulling the trigger should *not* dry-fire the gun.

If the gun fails to function properly through any of these checks, take it to a gunsmith. These are general function checks; you should consult your owner's manual for any unique checks for your particular gun.

Figure 74

## Loading a semiauto

Loading the magazine (often, *and inappropriately,* called a "clip") may require some manual dexterity, but newcomers will quickly acquire the knack (Figure 75). The owner's manual will provide guidance. Several manufacturers include a loading tool with the firearm. The manual will also indicate the total number of rounds that can be loaded. The magazine may have small, numbered holes that denote the number of cartridges loaded (Figure 76). Usually, the total becomes obvious when you reach the point where the magazine won't accept another cartridge.

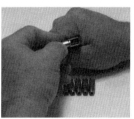

Figure 75

Figure 76

The magazine is inserted into its well—the hollow inside the grip—and pushed home until you hear and feel a click (Figure 77). Remember to keep your finger outside the trigger guard while doing this. Many experienced gun handlers give the magazine a tap with the butt of the palm to ensure that it is properly seated. You can do that, but it is not necessary to give it a heavy, melodramatic whack like they do in the movies. It doesn't hurt to give a tug on the magazine to be sure it is locked in place.

To chamber a round, make sure the gun is pointed in a safe direction, then pull the slide all the way back and just let it go. It will fly forward, strip a cartridge from the magazine, and chamber it. Be sure to keep your finger outside

Figure 77

the trigger guard when doing this.

Letting the slide fly forward ensures that the gun will go completely into battery (the condition in which the cartridge is properly chambered with the breach and barrel properly locked). The gun is designed to operate by having the slide slam shut during its normal operating cycle. Letting it do so will not hurt the gun in any way.

The gun is now ready to fire.

## Stoppages, jams, and failures to fire

The bad news is that semi-autos can jam. The good news is that newer semiautos jam a whole lot less than older models.

The bad press on semiautos and jamming probably comes from older guns that, because of neglect or misuse, malfunctioned with irritating frequency. Most modern, high-quality semiautos jam only rarely. And even then, many experts argue, the reason can usually be found in the shooter's technique, a faulty magazine, or the ammunition.

"Limp-wristing,"[9] can result in a "stovepipe."[10] If that happens, holding the gun more firmly when shooting may cure the problem.

Limp-wristing can also cause the slide to "short cycle."[11]

Many semiautos that seem to have a jamming problem will operate flawlessly if a new magazine is used. The feed lips[12] on magazines are subject to being bent out of shape, often from having been given too many heavy, melodramatic whacks like they do in the movies.

Occasionally, magazine springs weaken. They are easily replaced. Any buildup of dirt inside the magazine can also cause problems. (Magazines should be cleaned after firing, along with the gun itself. Consult your owner's manual or a gunsmith for instructions on disassembling the magazine.)

Certain semiautos just seem to like certain ammunition and dislike other ammunition. Undoubtedly, there are hard, cold technical reasons why a particular semiauto runs smoothly with Brand X, yet gags when

---

[9] Limp-wristing means not hanging on to the gun as firmly as it needs to be held when fired. This can cause some guns to malfunction.

[10] The slide does not fully eject the spent case, but rather closes on it so it sits upright in the ejection port. The spent case resembles a vertical stove pipe—hence the name.

[11] Short cycle means not to travel fully to the rear, which can cause a feeding jam. Or, the slide can fail to pick up a fresh round.

[12] Feed lips are the rolled metal or metal-lined plastic top of the magazine that holds the cartridges in the magazine.

fed Brand Y. You should determine which brand works well in your gun and stick to it.

Sometimes, a cartridge will be picked up but jam at the mouth of the chamber. If this happens often, and other remedies have been tried (such as different ammunition, different magazines, or a different recoil spring), the gun needs the attention of a gunsmith.

As with revolvers, if, at any time when shooting, you hear or feel anything unusual, if any one shot sounds, feels, or looks unlike other shots, *stop shooting immediately!* Perform a clearing procedure, then examine the gun and ammunition. Check the barrel in any of the ways described above to be sure there is no obstruction.

Also, like the revolver, semiautos may experience a hang fire. As with the revolver, the odds against a hang-fire firing after 60 seconds are astronomical, so it's probably safe to extract the round and ask a range officer what to do with dud rounds.

### Unloading a semiauto

A semiauto is designed to eject the empty shell case after each cartridge is fired. Nevertheless, when you discontinue shooting or run out of ammunition, you should still perform a clearing procedure. This is especially true if you stop shooting before the magazine is emptied.

### The "tap-rack"

Taught as a self-defense and law enforcement method to clear a jam, the *tap-rack* method involves two steps.

First, tap the bottom of the magazine with the butt of your palm (it's really a smack) to ensure that it is fully seated in the grip.

Second, turn the gun a quarter turn to the right (so the ejection port is facing downward) and rack the slide, pulling it back all the way and letting go. This will almost always result in any jammed cartridge or spent case falling clear and chambering a fresh round.

### Negligent discharges

You might think of "negligent discharges" as a fancy way of describing when guns go off accidentally. But guns do not "go off." They are always fired.

*Somebody put ammunition in the gun, then somebody pulled the trigger.*

This is an important concept. The idea that guns "go off" has somehow crept across the gulf between those who know nothing about guns and those who have broad experience with them.

Those who know nothing about guns assume that no matter where they are or what state they are in, they are ticking time bombs waiting to "go off" at any time. (Think of a lunatic with a meat cleaver who may at any moment start running around and attacking people.) Those who should know better sometimes use the phrase "the gun went off," despite knowing that guns don't fire themselves.

What they really mean is, "the gun fired" or, more accurately, "the person fired the gun."

This is not an issue of syntax. In the first place, "going off" supports the erroneous view that guns fire themselves. In the second place, it tends to blur the responsibility of just who pulled the trigger.

### Real-world examples

The following stories are true. Only the names have been changed to protect the foolish.

**Robert** was in the habit of leaving his .357 Magnum revolver loaded and hanging in its holster in the front closet. (Generally, this is considered a bad idea, as we discuss in the section beginning on page 131.)

One day while he was out, his father-in-law, Frank, came over to visit Robert's wife, Marie. Neither father nor daughter knew the slightest thing about guns.

As Frank was getting his coat from the closet on his way out, his eye fell on the gun. He asked Marie if it was loaded. "Oh, no. Robert would never leave a loaded gun around the house," she reportedly said.

So Frank drew the gun out of its holster and pulled the trigger. There was an ear-splitting report, and a hole appeared in the floor. Fortunately, nobody was hurt.

Comments:

There are so many mistakes here that we'll have to number them.

1. Robert should never have left a loaded gun where some unknowing and unsafe person could get at it. Those people included:

   - his wife, who knew so little about guns that she didn't even know how to check a revolver to see whether it was loaded,
   - anyone else who happened to glance into the front closet, including burglars, and
   - in-laws.

2.  The father, seeing a gun he didn't know anything about, should never have picked it up . . . and pulled the trigger!

3.  In addition to choosing a bad place to leave a loaded gun, Robert failed to show his wife the very simple basics of checking a revolver to see if it's loaded. However, since she was probably as resistant to knowing anything at all about guns, as many people are, he should have told her that it *was* loaded and that nobody should touch it. (That's not an acceptable substitute for having the gun properly secured, but it might have helped in this case.)

One other lesson this story teaches is what a complex, unnecessary tangle people get into because they have resisted knowing anything at all about guns. A glance at the gun would have answered the question and avoided the problem. But the father took the long way around, trusting his daughter's assessment of her husband. She decided she knew her husband well enough to declare with certainty that he would never, ever leave a loaded gun around.

What we have here is a cat's-cradle of people trying to determine the answer to a simple question by assessing each other's personalities.

To repeat: A glance at the gun would have answered the question. Robert's wife could have learned to check it in about five seconds if she wanted to.

And note that the gun did not just "go off." The father, apparently consumed with curiosity to know what an empty gun sounds like when the trigger is pulled, pulled the trigger. (He still doesn't know.)

**Kyle** owned two of the same model of handgun, the Glock Model 19. He had them both at his workbench for cleaning. He cleaned and reassembled one, then dry-fired it several times to be sure it was in good working order. His wife called him to dinner.

Returning to the workbench later, he picked up what he took to be the one he had just cleaned and dry-fired it again. Only it wasn't a dry-fire. He put a hole in his workbench.

Comments:

Easy. Kyle didn't perform a clearing procedure before dry-firing. As we said above, always treat every gun as if it's loaded until you have proven otherwise. Loaded until proven unloaded. *Always check.* Then do it again.

**Derek** was in the habit of leaving his Browning High Power 9mm semiauto in a desk drawer with a round in the chamber for home defense. Although some people feel its okay to leave the gun "cocked and locked" (round in the chamber, safety on) he didn't like leaving the gun that way. Instead, he adopted an unconventional approach, leaving the hammer on the half-cock notch, but with a round in the chamber. He reasoned it would be easier to thumb the hammer back if he needed the gun quickly than to have to rack the slide to chamber a round.

He periodically took the gun out and examined it, which is good. But that meant he had to return it to its almost-ready-to-fire state each time.

In order to chamber a round and lower the hammer to the half-cock notch by pulling the trigger and catching the hammer—an operation he rightly saw as hazardous—he came up with an oddball solution. He carved down a wooden clothespin so it could be inserted in front of the hammer, blocking its fall when the trigger was pulled. He had never heard of this being done, but didn't see anything wrong with doing it. The hammer would snap harmlessly against the wood, or so he thought.

The system worked a dozen times or so, but one day the hammer fell and the gun fired. Fortunately, this gun too was aimed in a harmless direction, the basement floor.

Comments:

What Derek had done, without realizing it, was to create what's called a transfer bar. When the hammer fell, it struck the wood as usual, but in this case the wood was touching the firing pin. The energy was transmitted to the firing pin through the wood (much like a croquet player who puts his foot on one ball that is resting against another and strikes it, sending the second ball off, even though it was never struck).

The technical explanation for why the gun fired is not important. In fact, Derek's real mistake was in assuming he could use a never-before-heard-of technique for lowering the hammer. If there's some well-established technique for lowering the hammer without firing the gun, then it's okay to use it. If not, it isn't.

Note that here is another case where the gun did not "go off." Derek didn't mean to fire it, but he did fire it. He loaded it, he pulled the trigger, and it fired. His action caused the problem.

Here's a little good news, at least.

Note that all three of the stories above ended in embarrassment or expense, but not in tragedy. That's because, in every case, the gun was pointed in a fairly safe direction, although that was not necessarily what the shooters intended. That underscores the importance of the first rule of gun safety: *Keep the muzzle pointed in a safe direction.*

## Safeties

The very word *safety* is misleading. It can make the shooter feel that he or she can relax and let a mechanical device take over the job of seeing that nobody gets hurt.

Let's get one thing absolutely straight: The presence of a safety lever, switch, catch, or some type of internal locking mechanism on a gun, and the fact that it is pointing at "safe," does not make it acceptable to violate the first two principles of gun safety.

The finger must always remain off the trigger until ready to fire, and the gun must always be pointed in a safe direction.

Realistically, it makes no difference. Those two rules must be observed with religious fervor, whether the safety is pointed to "safe" or "fire."

Some experienced gun handlers view safeties as potentially hazardous, ironic as that might sound. They reason is that reliance on the mechanical safety breeds neglect of the rules of safe gun handling. The excuse, "I thought the safety was on," rings hollow in the face of tragedy. Others, equally experienced, disagree. They say that safeties have an important role in helping to keep people from unintentionally firing their guns. In any case, safeties *can* fail. They are mechanical devices, and mechanical devices are capable of malfunctioning. We are not belittling safeties. For many designs, such as a single-action semiauto, a safety is desirable. However, the mechanical safety is no substitute for safe gun handling — *ever!*

Bearing that in mind, let's look at safeties as they are seen in the real world.

### Revolver safeties

Tradition holds that double-action revolvers don't need safeties because they have one huge, inherent safety feature: the long, heavy pull needed to make them fire.

Additionally, the hammer is initially at rest, not cocked and ready to be released, and not under any type of spring tension (Figure 78). The vast majority of gun-familiar people are

**Figure 78**

persuaded that nobody, but nobody, accidentally pulls a long, 12 to 15-pound double-action trigger.

Of course, when the hammer has been cocked, the gun becomes a single-action, with its light and very short trigger pull (Figure 79).

**Figure 79**

It might seem that a revolver, when cocked, becomes unsafe. But when it comes to guns, or any other mechanism, a point eventually must be reached where the manufacturer has no choice but to allow the thing to operate, because that's what the operator wants it to do. That point is reached with a revolver when the operator, having loaded it, also cocks it. Let's just say that anyone cocking a revolver must follow the two cardinal rules of gun handling.

Other types of safeties are almost unheard-of on revolvers: operator-engaged safeties—a switch or button of some sort.

But most double-action revolvers have two built-in safety features that work in the background without the operator engaging them or even being aware of their presence.

Consider what would happen if a revolver's hammer were unintentionally drawn back (caught on clothing, for example), and then just as unintentionally released. The gun would unintentionally fire. (In other words, it really would "go off" with no human intervention.)

To prevent that, many modern revolvers have an internal feature that will not allow the firing pin to project beyond the recoil shield if the trigger is not also being pulled (Figure 80). That way, if the trigger is left alone, the gun cannot fire.

Likewise, after the hammer has fallen and the trigger is released, the firing pin draws back behind the recoil shield and remains there even if, for example, the gun were to fall and land on its hammer.

**Figure 80**

You can observe these safety features for yourself. With an empty gun pointed in a safe direction, look through the gap between the back of the cylinder and the front of the recoil shield.

Pull the trigger and watch the hammer draw back. When the hammer finally falls, the firing pin will project. Release the trigger and note how the firing pin retracts. Now, draw the hammer back most of the way, either with your thumb or by pulling the trigger. Remove your finger from the trigger and let the hammer "slip." The hammer falls, but the firing pin will not project. Note also that, after the hammer falls, even a blow on the hammer will not cause the firing pin to project.

Another variation of these internal safeties is the transfer bar (Figure 81). In this instance, the hammer head is too short to reach the firing pin. The gap is filled by a piece of metal that moves up into the gap as the trigger is fully pulled. The hammer strikes the bar (remember the croquet ball), and the force is transferred to the firing pin.

A third type is the hammer block. In this instance, a metal part blocks the hammer from going all the way forward. As the trigger is pulled, the block moves down, and the hammer can travel to the striking position.

**Figure 81**

## Older single-action safeties

Some traditional single-actions are different. In the original frontier-model sixguns, the firing pin remained projecting after the hammer fell and the trigger was released. For this reason, the guns were not carried with all six chambers loaded. The famed six-shooter of the Old West was actually a five-shooter: one chamber was left empty during loading, and the gun was carried with that chamber under the hammer.

## Semiauto safeties

Semiautos have a bewildering variety of safety devices. They go up, down, in, out, and sideways. Many have passive safety features, like those found on revolvers, that prevent the gun from firing if the trigger isn't pulled fully to the rear.

Grip safeties prevent firing if the gun isn't being held properly. Other safeties block the hammer from falling in one position (safety), or cause it to fall without striking the firing pin when switched to the other position (de-cocking lever).

Others, such as the magazine safety (sometimes referred to as a magazine disconnector), prevent the gun from firing if the magazine isn't seated in the well. Magazine safeties can inadvertently render a firearm inoperative. That is why guns such as the Smith & Wesson Sigma, designed for the self-defense (or police) market, do not have them.

It's beyond the scope of this book to try to describe each semiauto's safety system. That's why it's vital for the owner of any handgun to get an owner's manual. If one didn't come with the gun, call the manufacturer and request one, then study it.

Although the following discussion is no substitute for obtaining an owner's manual for your particular gun, we can make a few generalizations about semiauto safety devices, with the admonishment that mechanical safeties are no substitute for following the rules of safety. We include them here just for general information.

The manually operated safety is usually a short lever on the left side of the gun, on the rear of the slide or at the top of the grip on the frame (Figure 82). If the thumb of a right-handed person can easily reach it, and it's not a magazine release or a slide stop, it's probably the safety.

Many semiautos are equipped with passive safety devices, like those built into the revolver. One is the grip safety, a section at the back of the

**Figure 82**

**Figure 83**

grip that depresses when your hand grasps the gun. When *not* depressed, the gun is prevented from firing.

The magazine safety, described above, is intended to save the person who foolishly thinks that if the magazine has been removed, the gun must not be loaded. As with any other safety, do not count on it to prevent the gun from firing.

Some semiautos have a loaded chamber indicator (Figure 83). Although not a safety *per se,* the chamber indicator was invented to remind the gun-handler that a round is in the chamber.

## Trigger locks and other gun-securing devices

A variety of storage methods have appeared in recent years. Owning a gun carries with it the responsibility to store it securely when it is not being used. For some gun owners, especially those without children, effective storage may be easier to accomplish. The techniques and devices for securing a firearm are as

**Figure 84**

varied as one home is to another. And the degree of physical security, as distinguished from educational security, varies with the age and maturity of the home's occupants. What works in a home with an infant doesn't work where teenagers are present. The gun owner must act reasonably in the particular situation. Many states have tough penalties for failing to store a firearm adequately.

**Trigger locks** (Figure 84) are viewed disapprovingly by many who are familiar with guns. When first introduced a couple of decades ago, trigger locks were claimed to be safe to install on a gun that was kept loaded for personal protection.

That was not true. Many guns could be fired with a trigger lock installed. Worse, the very act of installing a trigger lock on a loaded gun in some instances caused the guns to fire. They should *never* be used on a loaded gun. In any case, they are impossible to remove under the stress of a life-threatening situation.

Trigger locks can be defeated by a person with time and a few tools. We will not say how that's done.

**Cable locks** (locks that disable the entire gun one way or another) are also available (Figure 85 and Figure 86). Most gunmakers in recent years have provided these locks with new handguns. Manufacturers do this to add safety, for liability

reasons, and because of political pressure. Many states now re-

**Figure 85**

**Figure 86**

quire that new guns be sold with locks. The recommended use for these locks is to thread the cable through the gun's barrel, which makes both revolvers and semiautos unusable. They can also be used to secure the gun to some immovable object. They do, however, defeat rapid access to the gun in an emergency.

**Internal gun locks** are appearing on more handguns. These are integrated key locks built into the revolver or semiauto that lock the gun (Figure 88 and Figure 87). They are effective, though it is difficult to see whether they are engaged. Typically, the keys are small and are a challenge to use quickly.

**Figure 88**

The effectiveness of gun locks in reducing accidents is unknown. For obvious reasons, there are no statistics for the number of possible accidental gunshot injuries or deaths prevented by locks. That doesn't stop legislatures from requiring them.

**Figure 87**

## Safes and strongboxes

The best way to keep guns out of the wrong hands is by keeping them in a safe (Figure 89), if rapid accessibility for self protection is not an issue. If it is, there are a number of quick-open strongboxes on the market. Safes are just too heavy to move, and strongboxes can be secured to their surroundings. The happy result is that unauthorized persons simply can't take the gun and defeat the trigger or gun lock later.

Strongboxes come in a variety of styles and locking mechanisms (Figure 90 and Figure 91). Some can

**Figure 89**

be opened with a key, others have a manual combination wheel, and still others have a battery operated electronic keypad.

Please do not consider the back of the sock drawer or the back of the closet to be an adequate hiding place. In fact, the first three places you think of will be the first places a burglar, even an amateur burglar, will look. Children are also far more clever than most grownups think. So please, if you have children, don't use the sock drawer.

**Figure 90**

**Figure 91**

## Sidebar: "Is this thing loaded?"

It's that age-old question, and it is a question you should never have to ask.

Either you know how to check it for yourself or you don't. And, if you don't know how, you should not accept it or pick it up in most cases.

The author, like most people who have been around guns for years, has had the experience of showing a gun to somebody who asks, "Is it loaded?" You say it isn't, at the same time wondering why the person is ready to take your word for it. You open the action and show that it isn't loaded, although the person doesn't really pay any attention to what you're doing.

You hand the gun to the person, who then points it at random and pulls the trigger.

You are then relieved you made sure it wasn't loaded, and it leaves you wondering why you showed the gun to the person in the first place.

When receiving a gun you are unfamiliar with, you should ask somebody who knows the gun well to show you that it's unloaded and to show you how to check that it's unloaded.

In every case, if you're not comfortable with the gun, politely refuse to hold it.

Handling a gun safely is not difficult. In fact, it's very easy. Just remember to *always*:

1.   *Point it in a safe direction.*
2.   *Keep your finger outside the trigger guard.*

## Sidebar: Gun-cleaning "accidents"

John Smith, 48, said he was cleaning his gun in his apartment when it "went off," wounding his next-door neighbor.

Most newspaper reporters would see nothing wrong with writing that. Most TV newsreaders would read that on the air without even the flicker of an eyebrow. But to any person familiar with guns, that statement is as bizarre as *John Smith, 48, said he was washing his car in his driveway when it drove away!*

We all know that some important information has been left out of the car story. We know cars well enough to know they don't just start up and drive off.

In the case of the gun story, news accounts are handled by reporters, who are generally completely ignorant about the proper operation of a firearm. They don't realize that guns get dirty largely on the inside, that to clean a gun you have to take it apart, and that doing so will reveal that the gun is loaded. Nor do non-gun owners see any problem with the idea that a person might take up a loaded gun and confine his cleaning actions to rubbing the trigger so vigorously that it fires. Reporters, as the author knows from experience, tend to see all guns as being on the verge of "going off." They regard a gun in a drawer as likely to "go off" at any time, and one being cleaned is even more likely to "go off."

As we said elsewhere in this chapter, guns don't just "go off." Somebody must load the gun, and somebody must pull the trigger. In other words, a human being must operate the gun for it to discharge, even if the firing was unintentional.

Here is a version of the story that may come closer to the truth:

*John Smith, 48, had unloaded his gun and dry-fired it a few times. He then loaded it. His attention had wandered to the television set when a violent blast caused him to abruptly re-focus on the gun in his hand.*

*Smith then grabbed a cloth and some lubricant. When police arrived, he announced that he had been cleaning the gun at the time.*

Is that what really happened? We can't say, but the lesson is: Never dry-fire a gun unless you have just confirmed *an instant before* that it is not loaded. And, just in case John Smith was telling the truth, always confirm that a gun is unloaded before cleaning it.

But we're pretty sure John Smith was not telling the truth.

## Sidebar: Decocking a revolver

Most revolvers will not allow you to unload them with the hammer cocked. It is likely then that the time will come when you have cocked a double-action revolver or are shooting a single-action revolver and need to lower the hammer slowly and safely without firing the gun. This is called de-cocking and is outlined here.

1.  With the revolver pointed in a safe direction, place the thumb of the non-shooting hand (the weak hand) in the space between the frame and the hammer.

2.  Place the thumb of the shooting hand (the strong hand, the hand holding the grip) on the hammer spur and pull the hammer back slightly. The shooting hand thumb (the one on the spur of the hammer) will take control of the hammer once it is released.

3. Using the trigger finger (the index finger of the hand holding the revolver), pull the trigger and allow the hammer to slowly travel forward ever so slightly (maintain control of the hammer with the shooting hand's thumb). The thumb of the non-shooting hand remains in place as a back-up (Figure 92).

**Figure 92**

4. Immediately remove your finger from the trigger and trigger guard, placing it on the side of the frame. This allows any internal safety devices to re-engage.

5. Continue to lower the hammer with the thumb of the strong hand, removing the blocking thumb (of the weak hand) from the hammer's path only as required.

It is *vitally important* to release the trigger as outlined in Step 4 prior to removing the blocking thumb of the weak hand.

This de-cocking procedure should be practiced with an empty revolver until mastered prior to loading the revolver.

## Sidebar: Clearing procedure for a semiauto

The full procedure, as provided by the some experts and law enforcement agencies, is very thorough, as you can imagine:

1. Remove the magazine (removes the source of ammunition).

2. Briskly and fully cycle the slide three times (should unload the chamber).

3. Immediately lock the slide open (if possible) and visually and physically (with the tip of your little finger) inspect the chamber, entire breech area, and magazine well, verifying they are free of cartridges. If the slide cannot be locked open, hold it open and perform a complete visual inspection.

Notice that in Step 2, we said "should" unload the chamber. There are rare circumstances, such as a weak or broken extractor, that may cause a failure to unload the chamber when the slide is cycled. That is why Step 3 is so important: it verifies whether or not Step 2 did its job.

Here are some reasons why we cycle a slide three times during the second step of the clearing procedure. If the slide is out of battery because the extractor is not hooked on the base of the live cartridge in the chamber, the first cycle will not eject a cartridge. (Although this situation might be considered rare, it could have several causes, such as a feeding malfunction when chambering a round during firing, or an unauthorized person manually placing a round in the chamber, easing the slide forward slowly, and then walking away from the gun.)

But here's the real potential danger: cycling the slide only once will not remove the round from the chamber because the extractor is not engaged to it. In fact, this first cycle should put the slide in battery, leaving the gun ready to fire. (This is another reason why we keep saying "Finger away from the trigger.")

However, this first cycle did accomplish one good thing. Assuming a normally functioning gun, the extractor should now be engaged to the cartridge base. With the second slide cycle, this round should come flying out of the ejection port, probably to your surprise. The third cycle is for peace of mind; we want a clean cycle with no other surprises.

Now let's look at another situation: you pick up a semiauto with a fully loaded magazine and the chamber empty. Being human, you forget the first step of the clearing procedure, which is to remove the magazine. You now cycle the slide. All this will do, of course, is load the chamber, but if you at least remember to perform the second step properly, you will cycle the slide again. During this second cycle, you will get a surprise as a round flies out of the ejection port.

If you are now confused and perform the third cycle, a second round will come flying out. By now, you should be able to figure out that you messed up somewhere — you forgot to remove the magazine — but all is not lost. Simply start the clearing procedure again from the top:

1. Remove the magazine.

2. Briskly and fully cycle the slide three times.

3. Immediately lock the slide open, if possible, and visually and physically (with the tip of your little finger) inspect the chamber, entire breech area, and magazine well, verifying they are free of cartridges. If the slide cannot be locked open, hold it open and perform the complete visual inspection.


*And remember - Safety is your responsibility.*

# CHAPTER 4
# Shooting Basics

The overwhelming majority of those who are new to handguns have seen thousands of shots fired, but only in the movies. They have rarely, if ever, seen a real handgun fired close up. In the movies, people draw guns and shoot them as casually as you might flick a light switch. For newcomers, though, firing a handgun for the first time can be both exciting and intimidating.

Don't worry about being intimidated. We *all* tend to blink. (If you watch a "Dirty Harry" video frame-by-frame, you'll see that even Clint Eastwood blinks.) Newcomers to shooting often screw up their faces, clamping their lips together and grimacing when firing the first few rounds. Even experienced shooters will flinch at times. But, being human, we also adapt quickly.

**Figure 93**

## The dominant eye

Put both hands in front of you, arms extended, and form a small "window" with them, as shown in Figure 93. Look through the window at some object and, keeping both eyes open, draw your hands back until they touch your nose. Whichever side of your nose the "window" is on is your domi-

**Figure 94**

nant eye. When aiming with sights, this is the eye you should use.

A second quick and easy method for determining eye dominance requires two people. Have the shooter and a second person square off and face each other at a distance of 10 to 15 feet. The shooter then points his or her finger at the nose of the second person (Figure 94). The second person then tells the shooter which eye the pointed finger is under. That is the dominant eye. Try it. It rarely fails.

When shooting, it is not necessary to squint or close the other, non-dominant eye. Many people learn to shoot with both eyes open. But if you can't, don't worry. The brain normally accepts the information coming in from the dominant eye (Figure 95); it becomes easy to disregard the picture being sent by the non-dominant eye.

**Figure 95**

That said, using the peripheral vision of both eyes for a wider downrange view will help you shoot only when it is safe to do so.

## Strong hand, weak hand

Most people will choose to shoot with their dominant hand. For right-handers, of course, that's the right hand; for left-handers, the left. In shooting, the terms generally used are "strong hand" and "weak hand." The strong hand is the one you use when pulling the trigger. Don't feel sorry for the "weak" hand. It will have plenty to do—so much so that, at times, it may seem that it should get top billing.

There is no requirement, by the way, that right-handers use their right hand. If it's comfortable, try making the strong hand correspond with the dominant eye. Dominant right eye—try learning to shoot with a strong right hand.

In the end, use whichever hand is comfortable for you. If you are right-handed but left-eye-dominant (this is called being *cross-eye dominant*), by all means shoot the handgun with your right hand and sight with your left eye. Cross-eye dominance is not that uncommon, and there are very successful shooters who are cross-eye dominant.

## Sights

This is very important: Never bring the gun close to your face to get a better view of the sights. Recoil will cause the gun to move backwards, and it could strike you in the face. Some shooters have done this, resulting in very serious injuries. Hold any handgun at arm's length when firing.

### Standard sight picture

Sights are designed to assist in shooting accurately. The standard *sight picture*, the view you should have over the sights, is the one shown in Figure 96. Note that the front sight's post is evenly bracketed by the rear sight, in the exact middle of the opening, with the top of the front sight post level with the top of the rear sight. And the bullseye appears to be sitting on top of the front post. Replicate this picture, and your chances of hitting the bullseye increase significantly.

**Figure 96**

The sights shown here are called Patridge sights (sometimes incorrectly called "partridge" sights) and are common on handguns. Other types of sights have other sight pictures.

Some sight variants are open on the top, like the Patridge sights, but shaped a little differently. The rear sight might be a V-shaped notch. The front sight might be an inverted V, a polished bead, or a luminescent dot.

### Fixed sights

The front sight of any gun is, with rare exception, fixed to the barrel or slide. Some rear sights are "fixed," meaning they can't be adjusted

**Figure 97**

(Figure 97). A fixed sight will be on target at the distance, and for the bullet weight and powder charge, for which it is set. There is a commonly accepted "factory" load for each caliber used in setting fixed sights. For handguns, the sighted-in distance is often 15 yards. In terms of "practical" accuracy, the bullets will strike within a six-inch bullseye at any range from 1 yard to 25 yards, so the "fixed" nature of the rear sight is no detriment. Fixed sights, by their nature, are more durable and more reliable. This is why most military and police handguns have them. Accuracy at longer distances will require the shooter to compensate by changing the aiming point to account for the bullet's degrading trajectory (more on this is later). This means, for distant targets, you may find yourself aiming "a little high."

In practice, however, few people expect to achieve precise accuracy when shooting with fixed sights.

## Adjustable sights

An adjustable rear sight (Figure 98) can be moved up or down to compensate for distance, bullet weight or powder charge, or right or left

**Figure 98**

to align the sights with the point of impact. Although the general corrective action is to move the rear sight in the *same* direction that the holes on the target should move, the owner's manual will tell you how to adjust them precisely. If you have a used gun with aftermarket sights and no manual, you can generally find knowledgeable people — firearms instructors or gunsmiths — to show you how to adjust them. (Because adjustable

sights come in so many forms, we can't provide complete or uniform instructions.)

## Other types of sights

The sights described above are generally known as "iron sights" (even though they are usually made of steel), to denote their simplicity and low-tech nature.

High-tech optical sights, such as the *red-dot sight,* are commonly seen these days on handguns intended for competitive pistol shooting. From the side, they resemble a short, fat telescopic sight mounted on top of the handgun (Figure 99). Until recently, these sights actually didn't magnify at all, but simply placed an image of a glowing red dot on the spot where the bullet will hit. The dot appears to move only with

**Figure 99**

the aiming-point of the gun, not with eye movement. It is a nice targeting aid and will increase accuracy, but is no replacement for skill and practice.

Telescopic sights are also seen on handguns and look similar to a red-dot sight. Telescopic sights magnify the target to varying degrees and place crosshairs or some other marker on the spot where the bullet will hit. Telescopic sights on handguns are generally used for hunting and specialized target shooting.

Laser sights, the latest in handgun targeting aids, project a laser beam from the gun to the target (Figure 100). Typically, there is an on-off switch imbedded in the grip to turn the laser on. Laser sights, under certain conditions, increase the speed of target acquisition and are especially useful in dim light. Again, they are no substitute for practice. Laser sights can also help in practicing proper trigger squeeze, because every movement of the gun barrel is magnified and can be seen on the target. A laser sight does not compensate for trajectory at great distance. It will sight a level shot and can confuse a shooter targeting at a great distance.

**Figure 100**

High-tech sights, particularly the red-dot and laser, may compensate for a bad shooting position, uneven or unstable footing, or poor eye-to-sight alignment. Red-dot and telescopic sights need to be "sighted in" for distance, wind and round specifications.

## Trajectory: big word, simple idea

Let's use the example of a handgun that has been *sighted-in* at 25 yards, which means the sights have been adjusted so the bullet will hit the bullseye at 25 yards. The barrel is tilted up so the shooter's line of sight and the bullet's path intersect at 25 yards.

Gravity begins to tug on the bullet the moment it leaves the muzzle. The sights have to be adjusted to take that into account. The sight picture for a 25-yard target actually has the muzzle pointing slightly above the bullseye. The barrel is tilted slightly up so that the bullet rises, at first, before starting its inevitable fall.

The bullet's *trajectory*, its path through space, may intersect the bullseye on the way to its high point, right at the high point, or beyond the high point. All that matters is that the line of sight over the sights and the bullet's flight path intersect at 25 yards.

## Hearing and eye protection

Our grandfathers were right about most things, but they tended to think that shooters who wore hearing protection were sissies. Maybe they *were* sissies, but granddad also wound up deaf.

We strongly advocate being this kind of sissy. Wear a minimum of foam earplugs when shooting .22 Long Rifle cartridges outdoors, and "earmuffs" for every other cartridge size, indoors or outdoors. With really powerful rounds, such as the .357 Magnum, wear both earplugs *and* earmuffs. When your grandchildren whisper "I love you" into your ear, it is important that you hear them.

Although hearing seems to recover after each exposure to loud noise, in reality, some hearing is permanently lost every time. All but the smallest cartridges will cause permanent hearing loss, *and the loss is cumulative.*

Eyeglasses offer good, though not perfect, protection for the eyes from debris and hot gasses. Ordinary eyeglasses are not safety glasses. Look for safety glasses with a rating of "ANSI Z 87.1." Safety glasses are strongly recommended and should either be wrap-around or have side shields. Otherwise, wear safety goggles with the same ANSI rating.

Nobody ever looked back with regret on a lifetime of protecting his or her eyes and ears.

## Let's go shooting

Becoming a good shooter, like becoming a good golfer, is best done by learning it right the first time. What happens when you practice poor technique is that you will remain a mediocre performer. Golf is best learned by starting six inches from the hole with a putter, mastering first technique, then distance. In shooting, accuracy, success and confidence come through learning the correct stance, precise trigger control and concentration, first on close-distance targets. Master technique first and distance second. If done in this fashion, as with golf, your success will be quicker, more consistent, and more enjoyable.

## Know your target and what is beyond

It is a sad fact that people are wounded or killed every year because shooters fire guns without clearly identifying their targets and knowing what is beyond. Most of the time, these tragedies are labeled "hunting accidents" (a euphemism that does little to comfort the victims or their families). However, there are also cases of informal (or even supervised) target shooting sessions ending up in such a tragedy. So, just what is our responsibility?

The person who pulls the trigger is responsible for the bullet until it comes to a rest. It may come to a rest in a backstop a couple of feet beyond the target or gently tumble to the ground a mile or more down range, once gravity has overcome the power of the cartridge. It is the shooter's responsibility to know that the bullet will cause no unintended damage before stopping. If you are shooting in a wide-open area, you must know that the area is safe for the full distance the bullet will travel, and that the bullet will succumb to gravity or an appropriate object before doing any harm. If you are shooting at a backstop, you must know that the backstop is sufficient to stop the bullet safely.

Before shooting, understand your target and where and how the bullet will come to rest. If there is any doubt about how the bullet will come to a rest, then you risk a tragedy. Do not shoot until you know the bullet will stop, and stop safely.

## Shooting from a seated position

Shooting while seated at a bench rest is very pleasant and usually enhances accuracy. For new shooters, bench rest shooting allows for focus on the fundamentals of grip, aiming, breathing and trigger pull. In fact, if it isn't comfortable, you're going about it the wrong way. Rearrange the seat height, the bench rest, or your sitting position however you need to for comfort. If sandbags are available, pile them up so you can rest the butt of the gun on them and not have to hunch over to see the sights. You can also use a folded jacket to elevate your handgun. Even better is an additional soft rest for the barrel to increase steadiness and accuracy. Avoid hard surface supports. Vibration caused by firing from hard surfaces will lower accuracy and perhaps damage the finish of the firearm.

Once you have read about and then practiced grip, aiming, breath control, trigger press, and follow through (all described below) from the bench position, move to a standing, two-hand position. Like golf, it is important to learn and practice the fundamentals correctly.

## Holding a revolver

As we stress every time we get the chance, safety begins when you reach for the gun. At the range, you'll be taking it out of its hard-sided box or soft-sided pistol rug for the first time. Be sure to have the gun pointed safely downrange even before opening the case.

And, of course, keep your finger outside the trigger guard. Your first act after picking up the gun will be to perform the clearing procedure described in *Chapter 3*.

All handguns have different styles and sizes of grip (Figure 101). It is important to have a grip that fits your hand. The good news is that most revolver grips can be changed. When shooting for the first time, find a revolver with a grip that fits your hand comfortably.

**Figure 101**

**Figure 102**

It is time to start using some of the terms described earlier in this chapter. The strong hand is the first to grip the gun. That hand's index finger is the trigger finger. To achieve the proper grip, the "V" formed by the web of skin between the thumb and index finger should surround the vertical centerline of the back of the grip, which is commonly called the *backstrap* (Figure 102). Imagine a hearty, well-executed, firm handshake. Gripping the revolver is exactly the same, with one exception: the index or trigger finger is extended and rests along the frame of the revolver, just below the cylinder. The remaining three fingers wrap around the grip. The pads of the middle through pinky fingers should rest comfortably on the opposite flat of the grip. The pad of the thumb should rest com-

**Figure 103**

fortably on the middle finger at about the first knuckle. This is a proper single-hand grip of the revolver and the basis of a two-handed grip. You may need to make slight adjustments for comfort.

When properly done, the strong hand holds the gun as high on the grip as is comfortable without interfering with hammer movement (Figure 103). This is important because the proper grip transfers most of the recoil energy directly up the arm and makes control of the gun easier.

The two-handed grip is recommended. It is the grip used by most shooters. The weak hand's fold at the base of the fingers is placed directly over the middle knuckle of the strong hand (the fold runs the approximate centerline of the frame). The weak hand index finger is under the trigger guard, and all four fingers of the weak hand wrap around the strong hand (Figure 104). The thumb of the weak hand rests on the frame just below the cylinder. If it is more comfortable, the thumb of the strong hand may rest on the top of the weak hand thumb. Hold the gun *firmly* but not so tightly that your hands begin to shake.

**Figure 104**

## Holding a semiauto

Again, upon picking up the gun, keep it pointed downrange, and keep your finger outside the trigger guard. Perform the clearing procedure described in *Chapter 3*.

Some manufacturers of semiautos are just now beginning to make their grips adjustable. Even with this innovation, the grip of a semiauto performs more than one function. Along with providing a handle for the gun, it also contains the magazine. To a degree, ergonomics are sacrificed for function. That said, the basics are largely the same.

**Figure 105**

Again, the "V" formed by the web between the thumb and index finger should meet the vertical centerline at the back of the grip (Figure 105). The index finger is extended and rests along the frame just below the slide and outside of the trigger guard. The remaining three fingers wrap the grip (Figure 106). Because the size of the grip is dictated by cartridge size and magazine configuration (single or double stack), the middle through pinky fingers may not reach completely around the grip. If control or comfort is compromised, you may need to consider a different model of

**Figure 106**

pistol. First, try a semiauto with a single stack magazine. If that doesn't solve the control issue, a smaller caliber may be necessary. Check to be sure the controls—safety, decock lever and slide release—can be reached. This is a proper single-hand grip for a semiauto and the basis of a two-handed grip (Figure 107). Again, you may need to make slight adjustments for comfort. When prop-

**Figure 107**

erly done, the strong hand grips the pistol so that the slide will clear the hand and most of the recoil energy will move directly up the arm and make control of the gun easier.

Because the strong hand may not completely wrap the grip, the two-handed grip should be used. The weak hand placement is very close to that of a revolver. The fold at the base of the fingers of the weak hand is placed over the vertical centerline of the frame. The weak hand index finger is under the trigger guard, and all four fingers wrap around the strong hand (Figure 108). The thumb of the weak hand rests on the frame just below the slide. The weak hand thumb rests farther forward on the frame, al-

**Figure 108**

lowing the strong hand thumb to rest on the knuckle (Figure 109). Again, hold the gun *firmly*, but not so tightly that your hands shake.

Two final points on weak hand grip: First, some semiautos have the trigger guard designed to allow the index finger of the weak hand to wrap the front of the guard.

There is much debate as to whether there is an advantage in using this feature, because you may interfere with the

**Figure 109**

movement of the trigger finger. Therefore, few of the nation's top shooters use it.

Second, never allow your weak hand thumb to cross over your strong hand (Figure 110). The slide is going to slam back under full power when the trigger is pulled. If your thumb is in the way, it will be injured, up to and including being broken.

**Figure 110**

## Shooting from a standing position

There are several standing positions from which to shoot: everything from a classic offhand target stance (used by competitive shooters, up to and including Olympians), to rough-and-tumble, practical pistol stances used in self-defense shooting competition. For the beginner to casual shooter, the isosceles two-handed stance is the easiest to learn and the most practical.

The *isosceles stance* is commonly used by both recreational shooters and law enforcement. Square off, facing the target with your feet at shoulders width. The knees are slightly flexed. Using the two-handed grip, the handgun is thrust forward with both arms straight and brought up to eye level (Figure 111). Bring the gun *up*, not your head down. The isosceles triangle formed with the extended arms and the chest provides strong lateral support. The shooter (again, square to the target) leans slightly forward into the shot. Your shoulders should be just forward of the hip joint. This is a very natural stance, and is

**Figure 111**

the most frequently used self-defense stance, benefiting from our bodies' natural defensive reaction. The Isosceles stance can be used for both "sight" aiming and "point shooting."

## Aiming

Lining up the sights with the bullseye is not as easy as it sounds. Not only is your body constantly moving—breathing in and out—but the human eye is just not capable of focusing on both the nearby sights and the far-off target at the same time.

You have to focus on one thing and do your best with the others. That one thing is the front sight. If the rear sight is slightly blurry, and the bullseye is just a fuzzy ball (and they will be), concentrate on the front sight and do your best to maintain the proper sight picture. Keep the fuzzy ball on top of the front sight. The sights will move rhythmically so that a perfect sight picture reoccurs as you breathe. Don't fight the movement. Anticipate it and make it part of your shot timing.

## Breath control

Two facts of life: You have to breathe, and breathing affects shooting accuracy. Try this—while sitting, rest the butt of the handgun on a solid surface, using an isosceles two-handed grip, sight in the target so it is resting atop the front sight. Take a couple of nice, deep breaths. The target will rise and fall each time you inhale and exhale. The time to squeeze the trigger is at the bottom of the breath, when the diaphragm is relaxed after fully exhaling. You are not forcing air out, just exhaling normally.

## The trigger finger

From a safety perspective, now is the final time you can affirm that shooting the gun will only harm the target. The backstop is safe; we know where the bullet will come to a rest. It is now time to place your finger on the trigger.

**Figure 112**

The center of the pad on the tip of the index finger should gently rest on the trigger of a single-action firearm (Figure 112). Greater leverage is required on a double-action firearm. Moving the trigger finger so the joint between the pad at tip of the finger and the next pad gently rests on the trigger will make it easier to press the trigger (Figure 113). Remember though: the greater the leverage, the greater the chance of pulling the shoot. This is akin to hooking a golf stroke. If the trigger finger is properly placed, there should be a small gap between the base of the finger and the frame.

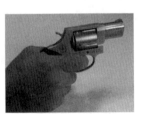

**Figure 113**

## Squeezing off a shot

Finally! After all this preparation—driving to the range, observing all the safety precautions, getting set, loading the gun, holding it properly, establishing a solid stance, taking a couple of nice deep breaths, performing a final safety check, and placing the trigger finger properly—*slooooowly* and smoothly squeeze or press the trigger. Do not *jerk* the trigger. *Bang!* The gun goes off and, with a little luck, the bullseye of the target has a nice clean hole in it.

## Follow-through

Like golf, you are not done until the follow-through is complete. You should see the front sight superimposed on the fireball created when the bullet leaves the barrel. You should feel the recoil. Don't fight it. Let it dissipate through your arms and be absorbed all the way down to your toes.

Recoil receives a bad rap. Although it is surprising to the beginner, you will quickly learn it has no control over your firing. As the recoil dissipates, hold your position, count to three, and then release the trigger to re-engage the action and ready the firearm for the next shot.

## Afterwards

After shooting, always be sure to "clear" the gun. Make absolutely sure it is empty, and then place it in its case. Clean the gun when you get home.

## In Summary

Each of the following elements plays an important role in becoming an accurate shooter. Starting with the list of pistol shooting elements originated by the NRA, we have tried to improve on their descriptions and bring forward the latest thoughts on each. Remember them and you will enjoy early success.

- Grip—Two-handed grip
- Stance—Isosceles stance
- Sights—Target resting just above the front sight—focus on the front sight
- Breathe in, out, in, out—and shoot at the bottom of the exhalation
- Slow, steady trigger press
- *BANG!*
- Hold your position for a count of three, letting the recoil dissipate, allowing you to regain a good sight picture
- Repeat

## Sidebar: Range basics

Most of your shooting will be done at a range. While we can't provide detailed instructions for every range, we can make some generalizations.

Common sense and the rules for most ranges require that guns be left cased until you're on the firing line. Also leave the gun unloaded until you're on the firing line.

Universal rule—although it might seem obvious, it's worth repeating: Always keep the uncased gun pointed downrange, no matter what. There are no exceptions.

### Outdoor ranges

At more formal ranges, there will usually be a range officer. In this case, do what he or she says. You can expect that all shooting, as well as loading and otherwise handling guns, will have to be done only when expressly allowed.

Periodically, the range officer will order a cease-fire so that people can check targets. During that period, if you are not downrange checking your target, you should not touch your gun in any way. You will often be asked to step back behind a line until the firing line is declared "hot" again.

At less formal ranges, the same protocol should be observed: Nobody should shoot or reload while anybody is downrange. Anyone at the range may call a cease fire for any reason. Listen for it.

### Indoor ranges

Indoor ranges are usually set up in such a way that shooters physically are not able to go beyond the firing line. Targets are typically suspended from overhead wire-and-pulley arrangements so they can be moved in and out. It's worth repeating: Keep guns unloaded and cased until you are on the line, and always keep the uncased gun pointed downrange.

## Sidebar: Is sideways cool?

A few years ago, movies began showing actors shooting semiautos while holding them sideways. We know no reason why anyone should do this. Obviously, some director thought it looked cool. Anyway, don't do it. The only effect it's likely to have, apart from making it almost impossible to use the sights, is to increase the chances of having a hot brass case bounce off of the top of your head.

## Sidebar: Long guns and eye dominance

Cross-dominance and long guns are a different story. When shooting rifles and shotguns, it is very important to shoulder the gun on the dominant eye side. For the right-eye dominant, left-handed person, this means pulling the trigger of a handgun with the left hand, and the trigger of a long gun with the right hand. The reason this is important is that the shooter maintains a better sight picture. The shooter is also more likely to have better judgment of range and speed when shooting at a moving target.

## Sidebar: More on stances

Modern handgun shooting stances originated in shooting competitions in the late 1950s and continue today. As in golf, improvements come from the same sources: competition and professionals within the sport.

Over the last half century, three stances have emerged: the Weaver, the Chapman and the Isosceles. All three have common elements. They all use a squared-off stance: feet offset, typically at shoulder width, with one foot behind the other to provide a solid platform. A "boxer's stance" is commonly used to describe foot placement. Obviously, the greater the caliber, the more important the offset stance.

All are two-handed stances benefiting from an isometric ("push of the strong-hand, pull of the weak-hand") grip to steady the handgun and improve accuracy.

**Figure 114**

The *Weaver stance* was developed by L.A. County Sheriff's Deputy Jack Weaver to improve accuracy at speed-accuracy target matches. Deputy Weaver began to win regularly with his new two-handed stance.

The Weaver used a "boxer's stance": gun side foot to the rear, with the knee's locked. The body is turned approximately 45 degrees from the target with the weak side facing the target. The weak side arm is tucked into the body and supports the strong side hand. The strong side arm is bent and pushes out; the weak side arm pulls in. The head is tipped to use the sights (Figure 114). The FBI adopted the Weaver Stance in the early 1980s.

A frequent competitor of Deputy Weaver's was Jeff Cooper, founder of Gunsite. Cooper's adaptation increased the amount of isometric tension and recognized the advantages of the Weaver stance in recoil management .

The *Chapman stance* was developed by Ray Chapman, IPSC Champion and founder of the "Big Four" shooting schools. The Chapman uses the boxer's stance, with the strong side foot back and the body at an approximately 45-degree angle from the target. The strong arm is locked out and straight. The weak side arm provides isometric tension and support similar to its role in the Weaver stance (Figure 115).

**Figure 115**

The *Isosceles stance* was popularized by Lethal Force Institute founder Massad Ayoob. Formalized in the mid to late 1980s, the Isosceles stance was the product of research into the human body's natural threat response. Captain Ayoob found that police officers under attack had a consistent physical and psychological response. He then developed a shooting stance that leveraged the natural and psychological fight-or-flight response.

The Isosceles stance is square to the target. Again, the strong side foot is a half-step back, with the weight slightly forward, shoulders forward of the pelvis, and knees very slightly bent. Both strong and weak side arms are locked out and at shoulder height. The head is level, and the arms bring the sights up to the shooter's eye level. A slight turn of the head aligns the sights with the dominant eye. The Isosceles stance makes the most of isometric stability. Neither arm can overpower the other.

We favor this stance because it is balanced, left to right and front to back. This stance is easier for cross-eye dominant shooters and for those who like to point shoot.

The *one-handed*, or *offhand*, position is the classic stance, and is required in some competitive shooting events. Illustrations from the 19th Century often show shooters standing with the strong arm extended straight out, head erect, looking down the arm at the gun. The body is perpendicular to the target with the feet at shoulders' width. Tuck the weak hand into a pocket or your belt. The shooting arm should be level and straight, with the elbow and wrist locked but not rigid. By definition, a competitive stance is not for the beginner. Work into this.

*And remember - Safety is your responsibility.*

# CHAPTER 5
# Selecting and Buying a Handgun

For many people, there is not one, but several reasons for buying a handgun. Target shooting, self-defense, hunting, "plinking" — any combination of these may be at work. In this chapter, we'll look at the subject broadly.

Recreational shooting includes some of the new sporting activities such as cowboy action shooting and practical pistol, and, of course, what is called "plinking" — shooting at cardboard boxes, pop cans, metal plate targets (from which plinking gets its name), and the like.

Handguns have been used for hunting at least since the 1930s. Many hunters like heading into the woods and fields with both hands free and their gun holstered on their hip.

People have purchased and kept handguns for personal protection since their invention. Consistently one of the main reasons for handgun ownership, it is also one of the most controversial, challenging the gun owner to contemplate a number of moral, legal, practical and psychological questions.

And then there's that hard-to-pin-down category that might be loosely termed "joy of ownership of a fine piece of equipment."

Whether purchasing a handgun for recreational shooting, competitive shooting (cowboy action or practical pistol), self-defense, or for investment or artistic reasons, there are common considerations. These include the level of quality and workmanship of the firearm, along with something we call "shoot-ability." Different for every person, shoot-ability includes characteristics such as:

- The type of operating system – revolver or semiauto
- How the handgun fits the user's hand
- The distance and fit of the trigger finger on the trigger
- The trigger pull – Is it too firm or too soft, too long or too short?
- Do you like the sights?
- The weight and size of the handgun
- The recoil – is the gun too powerful?
- How accurate is the shooter with the handgun?

If you have in mind some activity such as hunting or cowboy action shooting, you'll already have far more extensive ideas about what you want than can be provided here. If, for example, you're thinking about joining a group of cowboy action shooters, and they are using frontier-model six-guns, you'll take your guidance from the group. But here are the basics.

## Revolver or semiauto?

This is one of the big questions for first-time handgun buyers. For that matter, it's a perennial issue even for experienced handgun owners, who find themselves swinging back and forth between the two types. There is so much to be said for both types, that the author and everyone else involved with this book wiggled off the horns of this dilemma long ago by buying one or more of each. The number of new guns manufactured in the United States in the year 2001, the most recent year for which we could find figures, probably reflects the relative popularity of the two types. According to the Bureau of Alcohol, Tobacco, and Firearms, there were 623,070 semiautos and 320,143 revolvers made that year. That's roughly a two-to-one ratio. One reason for the larger number of semiautos is that both the military and law enforcement have standardized on these. Once those are accounted for, the general handgun purchasing population is more evenly split. Although there seem to be no statistics to indicate one way or another, most handgun owners will eventually wind up with both kinds, there being nothing exclusive about starting with one or the other.

## Some considerations

### The less frequent user

Will you be taking your handgun out at least once a month, shooting, cleaning and oiling it? Or are you more likely to put it away in a place safe from burglars and children, and take it out maybe once a year?

A revolver would be ideal for someone who plans to take it out of safekeeping only occasionally. We don't rule out a semiauto, we just lean towards the revolver in this case.

To put it another way, revolvers, because of their simplicity of operation, are a better choice for someone who is an infrequent user. Not that there's anything wrong with that!

We do advise firing, cleaning, and just generally going over any gun at least once every couple of months. Once a month would be better in order to keep perishable handling and marksmanship skills from deteriorating. Maintaining a revolver is simplicity itself, especially if it hasn't been fired.

The revolver can be left untouched in between those times, provided it's in a clean, dry place and has been given a very thin coat of lubricant (too much lubricant may lead to gradually clogging up the delicate lockwork inside). If the gun is kept loaded for self-defense, too much lubricant can seep into the cartridges and ruin them.

There is no downside to the revolver. If your interest in handguns increases at some later date, you can always add other handguns to your collection. Nothing about choosing a revolver brings you to a dead end. In fact, many handgun *aficionados* own revolvers almost exclusively, and many feel they are inherently more accurate for target shooting than semiautos. Some revolver owners say they have a particular gun that will shoot so accurately that it will create one ragged hole with multiple rounds in the bullseye at 25 yards. More power to them, we say, but that kind of performance is not confined to one type of gun.

Again, the durability and simplicity of the revolver make it suitable to the casual or infrequent user.

### The more frequent user

Are you more interested in guns—enough that you might be firing yours once a month or more? And, are you the kind of person who might enjoy getting to know the mechanism of the gun? In that case, the semiauto would be appropriate for you. It is more complicated than the revolver—for some models, quite a bit more. The semiauto will take a little more time and effort to learn to load and fire, as well as to learn the basics of field-stripping for routine cleaning.

Semiautos *should* be periodically field-stripped and re-oiled. How often depends on the environment in which the gun is stored. As a general rule, the more varied the environment in terms of temperature and humidity, the more frequent the maintenance. In the garage, get out the gun cleaning kit regularly. In a humidity-controlled gun safe, once a year or less. Some people may not care for the bother of periodically field-stripping a semiauto and cleaning it. Others may enjoy the activity. As we said, the choice is purely personal.

## Target shooting

Target shooting can be done with either a revolver or a semiauto. The only questions are how much money you are comfortable spending for ammo and how much recoil you are willing to endure.

There's not much debate, though, about the caliber of target pistol for a beginner. Almost everybody starts with a .22, and many stay with that caliber forever. Handguns and long guns in this caliber are by far the most popular. For handguns, both .22 caliber revolvers and semiautos are widely manufactured. The .22 has an awful lot going for it, and some of the most accurate handguns are made for the .22 round.

As a rule, the longer the barrel, the more accurate the gun will be. Longer barrels allow for greater spacing between the front and rear sights (sight radius), making more accurate aiming possible. And, in general, longer barrels produce higher muzzle velocities and, therefore, flatter bullet trajectories.

Handguns are not generally as accurate as rifles. Rifle barrels are longer, the sight radius is longer, and they are easier to hold steady. They also produce even higher bullet velocities.

Sights matter greatly. Guns intended for target shooting will always have adjustable sights. Different types of sights are discussed in *Chapter 4*, but for now it's enough to say that target-shooting sights are generally more sophisticated.

A word of caution: If you have little background with guns, and you want to get into target shooting, seek expert advice or find a target shooting league to join. Don't start off with a handgun with a type of sight that may not be right for you.

## Caliber

It should be obvious, but it still must be said: In general, the greater the caliber, the larger the handgun, the higher the cost of the gun and ammunition, the greater the recoil, the brighter the flash, and the louder the bang. And, to be realistic, at the upper reaches of caliber, the less it will get shot.

Handguns firing larger, "hotter" cartridges (rounds with higher velocity), such as the .357 and .44 Magnum, will kick (or recoil) more than handguns firing the .22 Long Rifle cartridge. You can shoot a .22 handgun all day long and it will not cost very much to shoot. A box of 500 .22 Long Rifle cartridges can be found for about $11.

Moving into the larger calibers, many shooters will grow weary of firing the .44 Magnum (think of Clint Eastwood's Dirty Harry character) or the .454 Casull after a half dozen rounds or so. The flash will be insignificant in daylight, but the muzzle blast and recoil pounds on the nervous system, not to mention the hand and wrist. The blast will be felt all over the shooter's face. And just one box — 50 rounds — will create a very noticeable dent in your pocketbook. Even those near a high-powered handgun will grow tired of the muzzle blast that accompanies each cartridge fired.

If it sounds like we're trying to ease newcomers away from starting with a Really Big Handgun, we are. We want you to enjoy the sport of handgun ownership from the beginning.

After the first "Dirty Harry" movie came out in 1971, Smith & Wesson found that their formerly obscure hunting handgun, the Model 29 .44 Magnum, which had received lukewarm interest from the public since it first appeared in the 1950s, was selling so fast that the factory had trouble keeping up with demand. An awful lot of those guns turned up on the market years later having been fired only a few times.

With its light recoil and low expense, we urge newcomers to start with a .22 caliber rimfire. If, in time, you feel like moving up to a much bigger round, you will have experience on which to base that choice. Recoil is also moderate with most 9mm and .38 Special handguns, especially those with a medium-sized steel frame.

## Complexity

There is no question that revolvers are simpler to operate than semi-autos — on the outside, that is. The revolver has a complex lockwork on the inside, but few gun owners will ever need to know anything about it.

The lockwork is behind an access plate held in place with screws. And, and unless you're an expert, that door should not be opened except by a gunsmith.

Semiautos are more complex. To own a semiauto is to commit yourself to periodically field-stripping and cleaning it. Its controls and moving parts should be as familiar to its owner as the controls on your car — steering wheel, gear lever, ignition, radio, air-conditioning, heating controls . . . you get the idea. You should also know the cause and cure of jams see *Chapter 1*.

In addition to the inherent complexity of semiautos is the complexity and number of passive and active safeties. These include everything from onboard key locks (now also available on revolvers), traditional lever safeties, grip safeties, passive firing pin blockers (again, also integrated into many revolvers), and recent, unsuccessful, efforts to create a technology which allows only the owner to operate the firearm.

In selecting a semiauto, particular attention should be paid to the position and ease of use of the thumb safety or decocking lever, slide stop, magazine release, and the degree of difficulty of field stripping. The first two are of particular concern for left-handed shooters, because the vast majority of handguns are designed for righties. There is good news for lefties, however. A small number of manufacturers, such as HK, are manufacturing ambidextrous semiautos, and after-market companies have always offered a variety of left-handed replacement parts. There are add-ons ranging from custom grips, a variety of different sight styles, and laser aiming technology.

Finally, a gunsmith can precision tune any quality handgun, turning it into a smooth, reliable and accurate machine with a surgically consistent action function and extremely accurate barrel and sights.

## Reliability

For obvious reasons, reliability matters greatly with any handgun, especially self-defense handguns. Revolvers have a long history of reliability, and there is no question that semiautos have gotten more reliable over the past several decades. Yet many handgun owners still feel the semiauto is still not as reliable as the revolver.

Here's why: The revolver is simple, at least on the outside, and it is *extremely* reliable. If you pick up a revolver and fire it a few times problem-free, then you can almost certainly count on it shooting thousands of more times without a problem, provided you take good care of it. And they don't care what brand of ammunition you feed them. It's all good, as far as the revolver is concerned.

The semiauto is very different. It has many moving parts, doing their jobs so quickly that the human eye can't track them. Improvements in performance aside, the complexity and speed of operation leaves some semiautos prone to jamming while others will perform perfectly forever. Figuring out which is which requires a little bit of homework that will teach you a great deal about semiautos. Jamming can occur at any time throughout the firing cycling, from the ejection of the fired round to the take-up and chambering of the next round. At the end of the day, most jamming problems can usually be cleared up quickly, and reliability improves after a break-in period of several hundred rounds. You may also want to experiment with a number of different brands of ammunition.

As a class, semiautos continue to improve, and individual handguns may be perfectly reliable, always functioning exactly as their makers intended. This is where quality and workmanship come into play.

You might ask after reading all this, "why are potentially unreliable semiautos apparently favored by the buying public by a two-to-one ratio?" It is because semiautos have other virtues. They have a greater magazine capacity than revolvers. With extra magazines, reloading is far quicker and easier. If this wasn't the case, the military and law enforcement would not standardize on semiautos. After all, they rely on their handguns every minute of every day.

Reliability is widely considered the most important consideration, if only because using a less than reliable handgun sets one up for a malfunction that may lead to injury. Buy reliability, whether the handgun is to be used for target shooting or as the service weapon of a police officer.

## Cost

Handgun prices vary just like any other consumer item. A new handgun from an obscure factory without an established reputation might sell for $100; a used one from the same maker for even less. A brand-new handgun from a big-name maker and with expensive add-ons might go for almost $2,000. In general, expect to pay $300 to $800 for a new handgun from an established maker.

The range in price reflects not only how much they cost to make, but the vagaries of supply and demand. The handgun market has its trends, and the price of a particular gun may reflect a recent increase in demand as much as it reflects quality and the maker's reputation. The .44 Magnum experience, described above, is just one example of the market's ups and downs.

Established gun makers with grand, long-honored names, such as Smith & Wesson, will always bring higher prices than guns from such completely acceptable companies as Taurus, which is not only a relative newcomer but an offshore brand. Taurus is a Brazilian manufacturer.

Although some favor American products such as Smith & Wesson and Colt, some foreign makers can command high prices for their products in this country. Sig Sauer and Heckler and Koch (commonly called HK) in Germany, and Beretta in Italy, have excellent reputations. Glock, of Austrian heritage, has also firmly established itself in America and dominates the police market.

Price also reflects the design and workmanship invested in the fruition of that design. Fabrique National (FN) Browning High Powers go for about $600, while the Hungarian-made version of the same pistol, slightly less well finished and with a looser fit, costs about $215. The $300 arsenal-refinished Argentine High Powers (licensed copies of the FN) are as solid as the FN guns in workmanship, but the finish is not usually as nice.

Suffice it to say that you can pay too much for a knockoff or lower quality firearm, but rarely too much for a quality handgun.

## Gun shows

For a real education in the gun market, visit a gun show. Visit several. The variety of items on display is astonishing.

The best thing about a gun show is that you can usually pick up and handle more different types of handguns in a day than you could in a whole weekend spent going from sporting goods store to gun shop. You can even try picking up the same type of gun but with different grips. Like a good pair of new shoes, you will only know if the fit is right by trying it on. There will also be plenty of good advice available at the right price — free.

If you focus mainly on handguns, you can really get a feel for what's out there, what's in demand, and what's the best-selling price. The majority of dealers will be FFLs — that is, holders of a federal firearms dealer license. Most dealers will have both new and used guns for sale. Often, the only way to tell if a gun is new is by looking at the tag. If a particular gun seems to have a remarkably out-of-line price, either high or low, and the reason isn't obvious, don't be afraid to ask the dealer why.

Any gun dealer worth giving your money to will be happy to take the time to explain a particular gun. If not, move on to the next table. If you don't like the price, move on too. Prices on identical items often vary by $100 from one side of the room to the other.

Besides gun dealers, there are always vendors selling ammunition, holsters, pistol rugs (zippered cloth cases), books, handloading equipment, magazines, videos, cleaning equipment, and military paraphernalia.

At the bigger shows, some dealers will specialize in one type of gun—for example, German military handguns from World War II. While these can be fascinating, we don't recommend making your very first handgun purchase a $1,900 Luger made in 1917. Your first purchase should be something practical, and probably costing a few hundred dollars.

## Gun stores

Gun stores are like any other store, only with tighter security. The salespeople will usually be very willing to give advice to first-time buyers. Their hours are regular and they'll probably always be there. Their prices are usually higher than gun show dealers due to their overhead. Full-line gun stores often carry all those neat little accessories for specific models of guns.

## Buying

Here's what to expect if you buy a handgun from a gun store, at a gun show or, for that matter, from any federally licensed firearms dealer (FFL).

Even before buying a handgun, some states require you to obtain prior permission from your local law-enforcement agency. (In Minnesota, for example, a *state* transferee permit or permit to carry a handgun is required. It takes five business days to process the transferee permit application, but it is non-discretionary, free of charge, and good for one year.) The permit to acquire is evidence of a state-directed background check.

At the store or the gun show, you will have to show a photo ID and any state-required permit, and fill out a federal form (BATF form 4463). The dealer will call an 800 number while you wait, and your name will be run through a separate *federal* instant criminal background check. The check usually takes only a couple of minutes. This is the famous (or infamous) Brady background check.

Assuming you meet all the requirements, you can leave with your purchase. **Note:** some states and local governments have a pre-delivery waiting period that could be anywhere from three to 30 days.

## Private sales

In most states, you can legally buy a handgun privately with no paperwork. In other words, Bob can sell his pistol to his friend Mark with no government involvement, provided the sale does not cross state lines. In fact, in most states, there are no forms in existence even to *record* the transaction. (Probably because of movies and books, there is a widespread belief that guns must be "registered with the police." Generally, not is there no such requirement, the police don't have any authority or even forms for "registering" guns.)

State laws regulating the purchase of firearms can be confusing and complex. In some states, if the buyer later uses the gun in a crime, there may be adverse repercussions for the seller (Minnesota is such a state if the buyer was, at the time of sale, a person prohibited from possessing firearms). Some local governments, such as Chicago and Washington D.C., prohibit handgun ownership altogether. Check with your state Attorney General's office.

## New vs. used

As with every other kind of durable goods, a new gun has certain advantages over an older, used one. For one, it will come with a factory warranty. There's also the sense of a new, never-been-touched gun that is pleasing to many people.

On the other hand, the price is higher. Count on almost any gun losing at least $100 in resale value the first time it's fired (we mean fired by the consumer — all guns have been test-fired at the factory).

Used guns often represent a terrific value. As the years pass, and the inevitable wear takes its toll on the gun's appearance, but not necessarily its reliability, a gun's value can drop to half or less of its original selling price. That's good news for used gun buyers, because guns are usually mechanically sound even if the finish is worn. However, a particular used gun might be a pig in a poke. Is it mechanically sound? Could it even be dangerous?

The firearms press frequently carries letters from gun owners saying they sent their handguns to the factory for repair and the guns were not only repaired, but gone through and tuned up, often at no charge. However, that doesn't mean that every gun will be treated as if it's under some sort of lifetime warranty. See the sidebar on tips for checking used revolvers and semiautos.

## Buying via mail or the Internet

Handguns can be legally *purchased* from out-of-state sellers directly via the telephone, mail or over the Internet. The *transfer* of physical possession, however, has to be completed through a federally licensed firearms dealer in the buyer's state. For example, say you have found a great deal with an out-of-state seller on a gun you have always wanted. The deal has been struck and the financial arrangement made. By law, the seller needs to ship the firearm to a Federal Firearms License holder in your state to process the transfer of the firearm. This includes filling out the proper federal and state forms (if applicable) and conducting any required background check. You should expect to pay a nominal fee for this service from the dealer.

## Different guns for different folks

Because there are many possible reasons to buy a handgun, and because different people have different needs, we've made up a set of scenarios. Here are some hypothetical examples of how a handgun buyer finds and then buys a handgun.

**Tom** has decided to buy a handgun primarily for home-defense. He and his family have a cabin on 20 acres of woods, and there are times when he hears strange noises at night. Coyotes are known to reside in the area.

Tom's dad was a combat veteran and knew a fair amount about guns, but because Tom's mother objected to having a gun in the house, he grew up largely ignorant of guns. He isn't sure whether he will get deeply involved in handgun shooting, so he doesn't want to make a major commitment of money or time.

Because of that limited commitment, the wise course for Tom is to buy something simple to operate, but with some degree of "stopping power"—a greater caliber handgun that may deter, wound or kill a larger animal, should he ever have to use it in self-defense.

A revolver in some medium caliber, such as .357 Magnum, meets these criteria well. Gun makers such as Ruger, Smith & Wesson, Colt and Taurus are known for making high-quality handguns, including revolvers. Tom can learn how to load, fire, and unload one through a basic handgun safety course.

**Figure 116**

Tom attends several gun shows and finally settles on a used Smith & Wesson Model 65 revolver in .357 Magnum (Figure 116). Because some of the finish is worn off, the price is under $300.

At an indoor range, he puts a whole box of .38 Specials through it and experiences no problems (.38 Special is one of the safe cartridge substitutes, as described in *Chapter 2*).

At home, he keeps it in a safe. At the cabin, he keeps it loaded with .357 cartridges and in a drawer that he unlocks before going to bed every night and re-locks each morning.

**Cynthia's** father introduced her to shooting when she was a child. She never had any interest in going deer hunting with him, but when he went to the range to sight in his rifles each year, she came along and fired his .22 semiauto pistol.

She got so she could shoot the bullseye right out of the target, and enjoyed it. But then she went away to college, got married and had kids, and somehow guns just never again came up in her life. Now in her late 30s, she and her husband have talked about getting into shooting. He's a former Marine and has a Colt .45 ACP semiauto. They've been to the range and she's fired the Colt a few times, but the blast and recoil are more than she cares for.

Although either a revolver or a semiauto would serve, she is fond of shooting rapidly and accurately. A semiauto offers the ability to get off quick, well-aimed shots. Although some legendary rapid-fire feats have been performed with revolvers, those feats were accomplished by legendary shooters. The revolver is slower to fire for most people. Cynthia looks at .22 semiautos. She can shoot one for hours for little money, and if she wants to move to a larger handgun down the line, nothing is stopping her.

After talking to people at the range, and doing some exploring on the Internet and reading a few gun magazines, Cynthia decides on a new Browning Buckmark .22 in stainless steel with a heavy barrel (Figure 117). Because the dealer has added a red-dot electronic sight and custom wood grips, it is in the $500 range.

**Figure 117**

There are kids in the house, so she keeps the pistol in her husband's locked gun safe.

**Rick** is an Air Force veteran. He served in the 1990s. At one point, his duties required him to be armed and qualified with a Beretta 9mm service pistol.

**Figure 118**

After all these years, he finds he misses it and would like to own a gun again. Although the Beretta is a fine pistol, he's a World War II buff and leans towards a classic Colt Model 1911A1 of that vintage (Figure 118). He finds, to his delight, that a friend recently inherited one from an uncle and has no desire to keep it. It's in very good condition, with a small amount of finish rubbed off from holster wear. Together, they look in a current copy of "The Blue Book of Gun Values" and determine that it's probably worth around $900, so they agree to that price.

Because the pistol isn't perfect, he knows that he won't harm its value by periodically firing it. While it's not exceptionally accurate out of the box—the guns were made as GI sidearms, not as precision shooters—he enjoys "plinking" at pop cans at his uncle's farm. At home, the gun is kept loaded in a lockbox that can be opened in a moment by pressing buttons in a certain sequence. The box is bolted to the top of the dresser. Rick's wife wasn't too crazy about that, but she reluctantly agreed that it was good to have the gun, and good to keep their kids from getting at it.

We hope these three scenarios will give the first-time buyer a feel for the kinds of decisions that ordinary people make about handgun buying.

## Sidebar: Buying tips for used guns

Certain truths apply to all used guns. If the gun is old but looks brand new, examine it closely for signs that it has been re-finished. The usual giveaway is that edges that should be sharp have been rounded off—a sign that rust was removed and metal polished before the gun was re-finished. It's no sin for an old gun to have been made to look new, as long as the seller isn't trying to pass it off as being in tremendously good condition for its age and therefore worth more money. Most gun collectors regard any "restoration" work on old guns as something of a sin. Pristine old guns are almost always more valuable if they are not re-finished.

By all means, check "The Blue Book of Gun Values," available at gun shows, gun stores, and the library. The Internet may also provide pricing information.

### Inspecting a used revolver

Check to be certain that the gun is unloaded by performing the clearing procedure. For a double-action revolver, close the cylinder and be sure it locks into place. Cock the hammer slowly and watch cylinder rotation. Also check to be sure the cylinder "indexes"[13] correctly. There should be little to no wiggle in the cylinder, once rotated and locked into place. Only a gunsmith can tell if the gun "indexes" perfectly, meaning that it lines the chamber up exactly with the barrel, but this test is pretty good at eliminating sloppy revolvers. Do this test on each chamber.

If the seller allows you to dry-fire it, pull the trigger and dry-fire it several times. You are looking for normal, smooth functioning. The cylinder will revolve and the hammer will rise and then fall, all very smoothly. When you release the trigger, watch to be sure the firing pin retracts into the frame properly, and check for a slight movement in the hammer, indicating that it has properly moved into position. This internal safety keeps the revolver from firing should it be dropped.

Swing the cylinder open and look down the bore with a light to check for wear. The bore of a gun that hasn't fired corrosive ammunition or that hasn't been fired a lot can be like new (although the bore may be dirty). An excessively worn bore is a sign that the gun has been fired thousands of rounds, which will reduce its price.

With the cylinder out on its crane, examine the chambers for excessive wear. Look at the area around the back of the barrel (forcing cone) for erosion, especially in a gun that fires magnum cartridges. Do the same for the top of the frame above the forcing cone. Also check to see if

---

[13] Cylinder indexing is the aligning and locking into place of a chamber of the cylinder with the barrel.

the crane pin[14] is tight by *gently* twisting the crane and cylinder assembly while looking at the crane pin where it enters the frame. Any more than a minute amount of play could mean eventual trouble.

Push the ejector rod to check its function. Now, pinch the end of the rod and give it, along with the cylinder, a rapid spin. If the rod wobbles while spinning, it is bent. Look under the ejector star for built-up dirt, which is merely a sign that the gun hasn't been kept as clean as it should have been. Close the cylinder and look at the barrel-cylinder gap against a bright light. You should see very little daylight, and the top-to-bottom clearance of the gap should be even. In other words, the cylinder should be at a perfect right angle to the bore.

General fit, feel, function, and appearance of the revolver are important, but subjective.

## Inspecting a used semiauto

Check to be certain that the gun is empty by performing a clearing procedure.

Lock the slide back and inspect the inside of the gun thoroughly. If the seller has no objection, rapidly pull the slide back and let it fly forward several times in quick succession. You are looking for normal smooth functioning, especially that the hammer (if there is one) doesn't fall without the trigger being pulled. Check that all safeties work. Check that the gun will not fire when out of battery by holding the slide slightly rearward and attempting to pull the trigger.

Lock the slide open, if possible, and look down the bore with a bore light. You are looking for wear and corrosion. Field strip the gun, if allowed, and look for wear marks on the underside of the slide where the disconnector mechanism rubs. Check for wear on the slide and frame rails themselves. Any wear should be even, all the way down the rail and on both sides. Naturally, when you're done inspecting the gun, put it back together again and leave it the way you found it.

Once back together, check that the magazine inserts and drops smoothly. Does the slide lock open properly when the magazine is empty (if the gun is so equipped)? Get a feel for the life in the magazine spring by using a pencil to force the follower[15] down into the magazine.

Again, evaluate the general fit, feel, function, and appearance of the

---

[14] The pin that attaches the cylinder to the frame
[15] The magazine follower supports the cartridges and acts as a spring cap between the spring and the cartridge.

semiauto. This is important, but subjective.

In *Chapter 4*, we discussed how a handgun should fit in your hand, the proper trigger finger fit, and other considerations around the fit of the handgun and your accuracy with it.

*And remember - Safety is your responsibility.*

# CHAPTER 6
# Cleaning and Maintenance

Many people find cleaning a gun to be a pleasurable interlude. They have the gleaming metal in their hands and are surrounded by the familiar fragrance of Outers, Shooter's Choice, or Hoppe's No. 9 solvent, reminders of childhood times after hunting, plinking, or target shooting. Other people find it an unpleasant chore that just has to be done, like taking the garbage out on a cold night or digging wet leaves from the roof gutters.

Either way, cleaning must be done for at least three very good reasons.

*Very Good Reason No. 1:* A gun is a finely made collection of precision components that just does not work well when it's dirty. Some guns are more tolerant of dirt than others, but in time, any machine that is neglected and allowed to become fouled will stop working.

A gun with a barrel or mechanism choked with debris can literally blow apart when fired, endangering the shooter and anyone else in the vicinity. That alone is a very good reason for keeping a gun clean.

Disaster aside, a gun becomes increasingly likely to malfunction as it gets dirtier.

A neglected revolver probably will continue to function longer than a neglected semiauto, but both types will eventually cease functioning when they reach a certain stage of neglect.

*Very Good Reason No. 2:* Reliability and safety are intertwined, but reliability really matters when the gun is used as a self-defense tool. If you are answering a knock at the door and decide that having your gun in your hand or in a pocket would be wise, you are going to want a gun you can count on. You probably won't need it, but if you do, it should be ready to function smoothly.

*Very Good Reason No. 3:* Protecting your investment. It's not uncommon to pay five hundred dollars or more for a good handgun. Cleaning it means not only keeping it reliable, it means preserving it, caring of it, and keeping it looking almost like new.

One of the remarkable things about guns is that, unlike most manufactured items, many guns maintain their value, and some will increase in value. In fact, old guns in excellent condition can bring startling prices. A Colt .45 automatic in excellent condition manufactured in 1915 can fetch a couple of thousand dollars. The new version of the same gun will go for about $700.

In general, a like-new handgun of considerable age from any major manufacturer — Colt, Smith & Wesson, Walther — will command a price far higher than was paid for it.

## Let's get to cleaning

You need a good place to clean a gun. A desk or table is just as good as a workbench. To protect the desk or table, you could buy a mat made specifically for cleaning, but there's a cheap, very effective alternative. Just take a big sheet of cardboard and tape a shop cloth or an old dish towel by its four corners to one side. Presto! A cleaning surface that can be used whenever you have a gun to clean. It will protect both the gun and the table. You're going to have a lot of stuff to put on it — gun parts, cleaning rods, bottles, rags — so the bigger the sheet of cardboard, the better. Two feet square would be good, and bigger would be even better.

When it comes to where to keep your gun-cleaning supplies, well, you could just toss everything into a cardboard box. But that approach results in a big tangle of cleaning rods, rags, brushes, patches, and bottles of solvent.

Make life easier for yourself by keeping them in some sort of order inside the box: rods on one side, brush tips in a jar, screwdrivers and other tools in an old cocoa can, and patches in their original plastic bag.

There is no need to spend a lot of money on an elaborate cleaning chest. A cardboard box works well, as does a toolbox or tackle box if it's big enough (the contents will only increase as time goes by, so don't start with a box that's too small). Just make up the internal divisions as you go along. Use cast-off containers from around the house. Baby food and pickle jars, or the bottoms of plastic milk jugs will all fit the bill. Use them to subdivide the box into compartments.

You don't have to buy an official cleaning kit, although they are handy. At an absolute minimum, you will need:

*A cleaning rod with screw-on tips.*[16] One tip has to be a bore brush of the right caliber (Figure 119). Another tip will be slotted. It's used to push a patch through the bore. You'll also need a brass "jag," as it's called, for the caliber you will be cleaning. When a patch is placed over the jag, it makes a perfect, very tight fit inside the bore, really reaming the dirt out. Many manufacturers supply a cleaning rod with the gun; some even provides bore brushes.

**Figure 119**

**Figure 120**

*Solvents* (Figure 120): Outers, Shooter's Choice and Hoppe's are among the major brands. Solvents generally come in two varieties: basic solvent (Hoppe #9, Outers Nitro solvent, and Shooters Choice MN7) or copper/lead solvent. Solvents are reserved for areas with baked-on residue from the firing process. This is commonly called "fouling." The copper/lead solvent may have an ammonia base for much tougher cleaning jobs.

Generally, neither basic nor ammonia-based solvents will damage the metal finish. Copper/lead solvent should be used only on the bore. Both basic and ammonia-based solvents should be used carefully and in well-ventilated areas.

**Figure 121**

*Gun lubricant* (Figure 121). Many solvents have gun lubricant as a part of their formulation. As the cleaning ele-

---

[16] Cleaning rod tips are made from a variety of materials: brass, copper, plastic and steel. Be sure to use tips made from a material that will not damage your handgun. As a general rule, softer metals and plastics are good bets.

ments evaporate, a thin film of lubricant remains. Gun lubricants are very good for cleaning all other "non-fouled" areas of residue. Also, you should keep a bottle of gun lubricant in your kits for those times when just a drop of lubricant is needed.

**Figure 122**

*Q-tips and pipe cleaners* (Figure 122). These will be used for hard-to-get-at places.

*Patches* (Figure 123). Yes, you *could* cut up an old T-shirt, but you'll use it up quickly. Splurge and spend a couple of bucks on a bag of 1,000 cotton patches. You'll be glad you did. Patches come in a wide variety of sizes. (Get the small ones only if you are cleaning a .22 or a .25.)

**Figure 123**

*A screwdriver that exactly fits the screws on the grips.* Using the wrong sized screwdriver will always lead to buggering up the slotted heads and reducing your gun's value. (However, some semi-autos have grips that should not be removed for normal cleaning, and their manufacturers say so. An untrained person could wind up in a losing battle with pins, springs, a misaligned trigger bar, or other loose parts. Follow manufacturers' guidelines closely when field-stripping a handgun for cleaning. Most manuals do not require removing grips for routine cleaning.)

*Glasses or safety glasses* to protect your eyes from spattering solvents or springs that can unexpectedly find their freedom.

Here are a few more items that don't cost a cent:

- Wipe-down cloth, liberally soaked in gun lubricant, can be used to wipe down the gun after cleaning. Keep it in a Ziploc bag. A second option is a silicone-impregnated gun cloth. Silicone will not damage grips or their finish (wood, in particular) and will leave a great-looking sheen. Gun solvents and lubricant can damage wood grips, causing a blackening of the edges as the wood absorbs these chemicals. It isn't pretty, so be careful.
- A wad of cotton from an aspirin bottle. Twirl the bore brush so the cotton gets woven into it. It will hold solvent nicely.
- A common wooden pencil with a rubber eraser tip.
- Common copper wire.
- Old toothbrushes. These are great for hard-to-get-at places.

*A word of caution:* solvents and sprays are *not* particularly good for your health, or for the health of your pets (including birds), so good ventilation is important.

The first step is removing the grips, if necessary, with your perfectly sized screwdriver. Wooden grips fare best when not exposed to the kinds of lubricants and chemicals you'll be using. As noted before, they will blacken around the edges. Plastic and rubber grips tend to be impervious to solvents.

## The truth about dirt & grime

First, understand that *inside* is where guns get dirty, Hollywood to the contrary. In the typical World War II movie, we see a group of GIs resting in a bombed-out building, wiping down their guns with rags, assiduously polishing the barrels and stocks. Don't be fooled; that isn't where the fouling takes place.

In reality, their guns would have been field-stripped (taken apart or disassembled) into smaller pieces, unrecognizable to most in the audience, and the soldiers would have been running cleaning rods down the barrels. But we'll give Hollywood a break on this one: many in the audiences would not have known what the heck the soldiers were doing.

So forget the movies. The dangerous dirt is on the inside.

Perform a clearing procedure as outlined in *Chapter 3.* Get used to hearing that said every time you turn around — Check first that the gun is unloaded before doing anything with it. It doesn't matter that you put it away unloaded; perform the clearing procedure anyway. It's a good habit to get into.

**Figure 124**

## Suspending the rules for a brief period

When cleaning, we have to suspend Safety Rule Number One, referred to in *Chapter 3,* during our cleaning session. After all, you can't run a bore brush down the barrel without likely pointing it in a number of unsafe directions. You'll even be looking down the barrel at times, which would normally be considered unsafe. However, you'll have to mentally suspend the rule just for this occasion.

## Double-action revolvers

Perform the clearing procedure outlined in *Chapter 3* and leave the cylinder open. That's about it to ready a double-action revolver for cleaning. It's a wonderfully simple gun, on the outside. It's complex on the inside, but you won't be going in there unless you're a gunsmith, and even gunsmiths don't take the access plates off of revolvers unless something has gone wrong.

Double-action revolvers are simple to prepare for cleaning. Take the grips off, if necessary, swing the cylinder out, and you're ready. You will clean the bore (Figure 125) and each chamber (Figure 126). Clean the frame and lightly lubricate the gun (all of this is detailed below). How much cleaning is needed? That depends on how much you've been shooting, but even more on whether this particular gun gets dirty from a particular brand of ammunition. Some guns rarely seem to get dirty, and a couple of passes with the brush followed by a patch or two will get the chambers and bore as clean as a mirror. Other guns get seriously fouled. Some people have fired hundreds of .44 Special 246-grain lead round nose bullets at 700 feet per second (fps) with no fouling problems. But shoot .44 Magnum 240-grain lead semi-wadcutters at 1300 fps, and lead fouling can become a problem. The dividing line appears to be about 1,000 fps.

**Figure 125**

**Figure 126**

With the cylinder swung out, examine the frame. Check that no dirt or grime has built up in any of the corners of the cylinder rectangle, especially the upper-forward corner. (When a revolver fires, some of the superheated gas and powder residue inevitably escapes at the barrel-cylinder gap, and it will build up in that corner.) A brush will usually remove the buildup. If it needs more attention, a length of heavy electrical copper wire can be shaped into a tool. Use a pliers or wire snipper to cut one end of the wire off at an angle. Copper is soft and won't damage the steel of the gun. The snipped end forms a small scraper to dislodge any build-up.

Since we're doing a little maintenance while we're cleaning, hold the gun up to a bright light and sight across the face of the recoil shield. Look for any metal sticking up around the firing pin hole. Depending on the model of gun, repeated dry firings will sometimes cause a slight bulge there that looks like a tiny dimple.

Because guns are made with such fine tolerances, a very slight protrusion there can result in the most unlikely of all revolver problems: a jam. The head of a cartridge (remember, we talked about that in *Chapter 2*) can catch against the tiny dimple. Should this occur, have a gunsmith repair the recoil shield. Then, do not dry-fire the gun without dummy rounds, or "snap-caps," as they are called.

Apply solvent to all fouled areas of the gun. Avoid spraying wood (if you haven't removed the grips) and any markings on the sights. During shooting, the byproducts of ignition get blown all over the gun, particularly around the muzzle and the barrel/cylinder gap.

The amount of cleaning and the tools needed are dictated by two conditions. First, consult your owner's manual. Some, like Glock, recommend against using of any type of metal brush. Follow any specific cleaning instructions offered in the manual. Second, how dirty is the gun? Generally, gun cleaning should take a minimalist approach, so start with basic solvents, a jag, and cleaning patches. Leave the metal brushes and ammonia-based solvents for use only when needed. The object is to get the handgun clean without doing any damage to it. To clean a revolver:

- Connect the slotted cleaning rod tip to the rod.
- Soak a patch[17] with cleaning solvent and run it through the bore several times. Then let the gun sit for five to ten minutes.
- Take the jag, attach it to the cleaning rod, and fit a cleaning patch over the tip (Figure 127).

**Figure 127**

- Run the jag and the cleaning patch through the bore. Use both sides of the patch, and use three or four patches.
- If the patches are coming out dry and dirty, apply more solvent, let the gun soak, and repeat the jag and patch process.
- If the patches are coming out clean, inspect the bore. It should be shiny to the point of being reflective and without dark spots.
- Use this same basic solvent process on each of the chambers in the cylinder.

---

[17] Practice is the only way to know how many times to fold a patch to fit snugly through the bore. Too thick, and it's like threading a needle with a shoe lace. To thin, and you are wasting your time.

- The only other part that is accessible with the cylinder swung out is the ejector star, which is held in place with spring pressure. Using the ejector rod, push it out and apply lubricant underneath with a Q-tip. A toothbrush comes in handy for cleaning the backside of the

Figure 128

ejector star and the rear face of cylinder (Figure 128). A lubricant-covered cloth will do a good job on the outside of the cylinder and the frame.

- Close the cylinder so you can cock the hammer (Figure 129). Use a lubricant-soaked Q-tip to get at as much of the action mechanism as possible. Wiggle the Q-tip into the action to loosen dirt. Use either a clean Q-tip or a screwdriver with a patch over the tip to clean up residue

Figure 129

from the action. Wipe all the residue off the gun with a soft paper towel. Use a lubricant-soaked Q-tip to apply a thin coat of lubricant to the action mechanism.

- Use a lightly solvent-coated toothbrush to clean the inside of the cylinder rectangle and the breach face/recoil shield (Figure 130).

Figure 130

- Then, go over the gun with your lubricant-soaked cloth. Go over all of the gun, including the area under the grips, if removed. Follow this with a clean, absorbent cloth and remove all the visible lubricant. Periodically, you can add *one drop* of lubricant to the base of the hammer, so it runs down inside the mechanism. Don't overdo it. Gunsmiths often observe that the only thing wrong with some revolvers is that someone has been squirting lubricant into the mechanism, clogging it up.

- Put the grips back on, if removed, and, touching the metal as little as possible, hold the gun by the grips and put it in its case or pistol rug.

**Is the bore still dirty?**

Repeat the process above using solvent and a patch-covered jag. If the bore remains dirty, use solvent and the bore brush. You don't want it dripping on your desk, table, or anything else, so do the cleaning over old newspapers that can be thrown away when you're done. Dip the bore brush and its shroud of aspirin-bottle cotton in the solvent. Run the brush *all the way through* before pulling back. Do not stop partway through and then back up; that can damage the bristles by doubling them back on themselves, whether they are made of plastic, brass or steel. Follow the bore brush process with the cloth-covered jag. You want to get all of the solvent out of the bore. Finally, run the slotted cleaning rod head and a clean patch through the bore. Put a few drops of lubricant on a clean patch and run it though the bore and chambers.

Patches come out dirty, of course, but you don't need to throw them away after one pass. Here's a cheapskate tip: If you use the bigger patches, you can simply reposition the patch slightly on the jag for each additional pass through the bore, or turn it over and use the cleaner side. There is no point in wasting clean cotton that's already soaked in solvent.

## Cowboy-style single-action revolvers

Begin by performing the clearing procedure outlined in *Chapter 3*. Follow the manual's instructions and pull out the cylinder base pin so the cylinder comes out completely.

Follow the same general approach to cleaning as for the double-action revolver. The manual will explain how to remove the grips, if necessary. Instead of an ejector star, there is an ejector rod under the barrel. If it has gotten dirty, check the manual for cleaning guidelines.

The cleaning procedure with solvent, jag, and lubricant on the chambers and the bore is the same as described above, as is the final cleanup.

Once reassembled, be sure the cylinder rotates and indexes correctly. The cylinder should lock in at each chamber and rotate smoothly. If it doesn't—off to the gunsmith you go.

## Semiautomatic pistols

Perform the clearing procedure as outlined in *Chapter 3*.

Your owner's manual will have detailed instructions for disassembling the gun, a procedure also known as field-stripping or takedown. The procedure varies with each manufacturer, and often from model to model in the same line. (Technically, disassembly means completely taking it apart, down to every last little pin and screw. Only gunsmiths need to do that.) If you don't have an owner's manual to guide you through standard field-stripping, call the manufacturer's toll-free 800 number given at the back of this book. They will be delighted to send you one, and for free. It makes their lawyers happy.

You can also visit your local library. It will have books on field-stripping and disassembling many types of handguns. Gun shows and the Internet are also good sources. Using a search engine such as Yahoo or Google, type in, for example, *colt model m pocket pistol takedown instructions.* You will get lots of hits, and frequently there will even be a downloadable printable version of the manual with illustrations, exactly as written by the manufacturer.

Virtually all semiautos break down into several large subcomponents: the frame (including parts of the action), the slide (which includes the barrel, recoil spring with the guide rod), and the magazine (Figure 131). If the semiauto is so designed, remove the barrel, recoil spring and recoil spring guide rod from the slide. Remove the grips, if applicable. Go ahead and apply lubricant to all residue-covered surfaces. We will deal with each of them in turn.

**Figure 131**

The semiauto is more complicated, and more of it gets dirty. You can — in fact, you must — really get inside the semi-auto to clean it. Every time it fires, the inside is showered with powder residue. It's not just the bore, but the whole interior of the gun that gets dirty, much more so than a revolver. Unlike a revolver, a semi-auto opens itself up like a big mouth, and then snaps shut on all the ignition byproducts. They find their way inside the magazine, into the recoil-spring area, and even underneath the hammer and inside the firing-pin channel. Pipe cleaners will let you get at narrow places, such as down the firing-pin tunnel and under the hammer. Do not throw Q-tips away when they've become dirty. Use a nail clipper to lop off the head. This will leave you with a sharp, tough little instrument for digging into small spaces. The slotted tip on the cleaning rod can be wrapped with a big patch and used to pry into interior spaces.

As with the revolver, give the barrel special attention: solvent, cleaning cloth and jag, and finally a clean patch with lubricant. Again, save the bore brush and any solvent for extra tough cleaning problems. To clean a semiauto:

- Soak a patch[18] with cleaning solvent and run it through the bore several times (Figure 132). Then let the gun sit for five to ten minutes.

**Figure 132**

- Take the jag and fit a cleaning patch over the tip (Figure 133).

- Run the jag and the cleaning patch through the bore. Use both sides of the patch, and use three or four patches.

**Figure 133**

- If the patches are coming out dry and dirty, apply more solvent, let the gun soak, and then repeat the jag and patch process.
- If the patches are coming out clean, inspect the bore. It should be shiny to the point of being reflective and without dark spots.
- Use the lubricant and a Q-tip/patch to clean the inside of the barrel channel of the slide, slide channels, and all other surfaces and crannies of the slide (Figure 134). Use basic solvent and a toothbrush on the breech face and extractor claw, followed with a Q-tip/cloth.

**Figure 134**

- Turn to the frame. The inside of the entire frame will need clean-

---

[18] Practice is the only way to know how many times to fold a patch to fit snugly through the bore. Too thick, and it's like threading a needle with a shoe lace. To thin, and you are wasting your time.

ing. Lubricant and a toothbrush, Q-tip/patch, and a clean cloth will take care of 90% of the surfaces.As you look down the magazine well from the top (Figure 136), you see that the trigger mechanism is connected to the rest of the action by the drawbar (typically running down the right

Figure 136

side of the inside of the frame). On the left inside of the frame of many semiautos is the slide stop. At the rear of the frame is the hammer, beneath which are the main components of the action. Along with the lubricant, toothbrushes, Q-tips, your screw-driver, and cleaning patches will be needed to get into all the crevices of the frame (Figure 135). Clean with solvent, and then wipe all surfaces. Cleaning the frame is a challenge. Rarely can you get into every corner or wipe every surface. That's just the way it is. Do the best you can.

Figure 135

- Clean the magazine. Disassemble it if you can (check the owners manual). Otherwise, use the eraser end of the pencil (we told you it would come in handy) to depress the magazine spring, pushing down on the follower[19], while running a lubricant-soaked patch (threaded through a slotted rod tip) all around in-side the magazine. Note how dirty it comes out. On magazines, use lubricant only. Never use solvents, because they can work into the cartridge primer and ruin it. Wipe the inside of the magazine clean of any liquids with a dry patch or cloth.
- When you're done cleaning and before reassembling the gun, wipe away any excess lubricant with a clean cloth. Leave only a thin film of lubricant. Add a small amount of lubricant to the slide rails, recoil spring, and guide rod, and areas of the barrel that come in contact with the slide. Lightly lubricate the inside of the bore with a patch to protect the rifling. Go over the outside before putting the grips back on. Be very sparing in applying lu-bricant to those surfaces where grips will be in contact with the

---

[19] The follower is the metal spring cap supporting the ammunition in the semiauto magazine. When the magazine is empty, the follower will be at the top of the inside of the magazine.

gun. Also be very sparing with lubricant in the areas that will be in contact with ammunition. After reassembly, go over the entire pistol again with a clean absorbent cloth and remove all visible lubricant.

- After reassembly, perform a "functional check," including disconnector, safeties, slide lock, going into and out of battery, and seating of the magazine. Dry fire the gun several times.
- Put the grips back on and, touching the metal as little as possible, hold the gun by the grips and put it in its case or pistol rug.
- Periodically, you can add *one drop* of lubricant to the base of the hammer, so it runs down inside the mechanism. Don't overdo it. Gunsmiths often observe that the only thing wrong with some semiautos is that someone has been squirting lubricant into the mechanism, it up.

You're done.

## Ammunition

The ammunition needs to be cleaned. Although ammunition left in its box probably won't need any attention (although there's no harm in looking it over from time to time), ammo left in the gun will probably become oily and must be cleaned periodically as part of general maintenance. Do not allow fluids of any kind to remain on cartridges. A soft, absorbent cloth or paper towel will suffice.

If the gun has been carried next to your body, ammunition may start to acquire a patina of corrosion. Inspect it closely. If it can't be cleaned up with a cloth, discard it. Check with a gun store or range for proper disposal advice. But ammunition acquiring a patina is also a sign that you need to go to the range more.

## Maintenance

Good news: Most of the maintenance for any handgun is simply cleaning and oiling the gun. Cleaning any object, whether it's a gun, a car, or a microwave oven, naturally involves inspecting it, so if there's anything wrong you will probably discover it during the cleaning.

If you find anything amiss, do not shoot the gun. Take it to a gunsmith.

Perform the clearing procedure, ensuring that there's no ammunition in it, and dry-fire it a couple of times if the owner's manual approves. Otherwise, use snap-caps. What you are looking for is the smooth, normal functioning of the gun. Check each of its features by performing a functional check.

You can now put the gun away, satisfied that you've taken care of your investment.

Be sure to wash your hands. Those solvents tend to be toxic.


*And remember - Safety is your responsibility.*

# Chapter 7
# Keeping, Transporting, Storing and the Law

Keeping a gun in the house, taking one outside your home, transporting one in a car, traveling by air, and carrying in general — all call for knowing the law.

But because safety is our first concern — coming even before legalities — we will give that precedence. Unless you are keeping a handgun for home defense or carrying one for personal protection, there is no reason the gun should be loaded, either at home or when being transported.

And whether the gun is loaded or not, always follow the two cardinal rules of safety: *keep the gun pointed in a safe direction, and keep your finger outside the trigger guard.* That will guarantee that the gun won't be unintentionally fired.

## Legal restrictions

First, if you have a permit to carry, the laws of almost every state allow you not only to keep a gun in the home, but to carry a gun almost everywhere, except in certain defined places such as schools or government buildings.

Over 70% of states have passed what are called "shall-issue" laws. These laws allow the states' citizens to carry handguns if they meet several criteria, such as being old enough, completing a course covering permit-to-carry issues and, naturally, having no criminal history, mental problems, or history of drug or alcohol abuse. If you reside in a permit-to-carry state, consult the Attorney General's office for guidance in carrying, transporting or storing a handgun. Even with a permit to carry, there may be penalties for improper storage. In Minnesota, for example, it is a crime to leave a handgun where a minor could gain easy access.

Now we'll discuss legalities for that majority of gun owners who don't have carry permits.

## Owning a handgun

In *Chapter 5*, we explain that it's legal in most jurisdictions for a non-felon who is old enough and has passed the federally mandated background check to buy and own a handgun. Individual states may also require a background check or, as in New York City, a license to even own a handgun. In most jurisdictions, it is legal to keep a gun in the home and, in many, at your place of business. Again, localities do vary, so check the law in your area. Don't assume that the Western states are universally gun-friendly and that the Eastern states are not. Vermont, for example, is very gun-friendly, allowing its residents—except those who are felons or are otherwise ineligible—to carry a handgun without a permit. California has a patchwork of laws, by county, that range from handgun friendly to onerous.

The simplest approach for most people is to go online and check the relevant sections of www.nraila.org or www.packing.org, both of which offer plain-English versions of state gun laws and try to keep as up-to-date as possible. While both of these sites are unabashedly pro-gun, neither has any reason to mislead people about state laws. In fact, it is in their interest to be as accurate as possible. That doesn't mean the law hasn't changed since the Web sites were last updated, however. Your local library can also be very helpful in directing you to state statutes. However, the library's information is unlikely to be as up-to-date as the websites'. Again, the Attorney General's office or a local lawyer specializing in firearms law are the best resources.

In Minnesota, for example, a gun-owning acquaintance told the author that the law requires the gun and ammunition to be at opposite ends of any vehicle. In reality, no such statute can be found in Minnesota law.

## "Registering" guns

Thanks to the movies and television, there is a widely held belief that guns have to be "registered with the police," or with other authorities, to be legally owned. In most states, that is just not the case. Unfortunately, gun registration is required by some states or through municipal ordinance. Check with either the Attorney General's office or the city or county attorney's office.

It is a good idea to inventory your firearms and keep serial numbers. Store your firearms safely and keep the serial numbers separate, just in case your guns are stolen or lost in a fire.

## Storing in the home

Firearms need to be kept from children, burglars, the emotionally unstable, and anyone else who should not have access. When it comes to children, do not underestimate their curiosity or ability to guess where a gun might be hidden.

We do not suggest hiding places as viable for storage. If individual gun owners choose to find, make, or build a place that is unlikely to be searched by a burglar, that is his or her business. However, we firmly recommend the use of a safe or a strongbox (pictured here), even in a home with no small children.

Sturdy steel boxes made specifically for storing one or two handguns can be purchased for under $100. The less expensive ones open with a key or a combination dial. Pricier version open with a sequence of strokes on a keypad.

If you are reasonably handy with common tools, you can install a strongbox in a readily accessible place. For example, you could bolt a strongbox to the top of a dresser so a burglar could steal it only by taking the entire dresser. It can also be bolted to an interior wall or secured in other ways.

Guns also need to be protected from humidity, so store them in a place not subjected to moisture or drastic temperature swings. Garages and unfinished basements are not good storage areas.

Ammunition, too, should be stored safe

from unwanted access in boxes that clearly identify the caliber (to avoid an accident of misloading a handgun). And, like guns, ammunition does not respond well to humidity.

As noted, states may have specific laws regarding storage and access by minors (generally those under age 18). Your local dealer or the Attorney General's office can inform you of any applicable laws.

## Transporting

Favoring safety whenever possible, we recommend keeping and transporting guns in an unloaded state if you're not carrying for personal defense.

**Figure 137**

Keeping a handgun in a case, bag, pistol rug (Figure 137), or other sturdy, closeable container designed for a handgun also makes sense. Three concerns dominate: (1) keeping the gun from prying eyes, (2) keeping it out of the wrong hands, and (3) protecting it so it doesn't get damaged and lose functional reliability or value. A gun left uncased on the seat of a car might be legal in some states, but it's not the brightest thing to do. It invites having your car broken into and the gun stolen. If the law does not require that the gun be kept in a container, hide it out of sight.

Generally, if you are allowed to possess a firearm at your point of departure and at your destination, you may travel with the firearm unloaded and encased from departure point to destination. This sounds legalistic (and it is), because some arrival points are very restrictive. Washington D.C., New York City, Chicago, and the State of Massachusetts all have very restrictive laws that could easily land you in jail should you arrive with a firearm. States may still regulate possession standards. The Volkmer-McClure act of 1986 (18US Code section 926A)[20] provides for "peaceable journey" when transporting a firearm. Forewarned is forearmed—check before you transport.

## Home to car

Check the laws in your state. In most states, it is legal to transport an *unloaded* firearm in a closed container to your car. But what's a "closed container"? States vary in their definitions but, in many cases, a zipped-

---

[20] See Appendix C.

up pistol rug, a hard-sided pistol case, or the hard-sided box the gun came in when new will meet the legal definition.

That gets the gun to the vehicle. And, after you have driven somewhere, out again.

## Inside the vehicle

Now comes another tricky part. Where in the vehicle may the gun be transported? Some states require the gun be in the trunk or the rearmost part of the vehicle. Other states do not. Let's look at some rules for several states as they apply to people without permits to carry.

This review is not comprehensive and is presented here to give you a feel for the variety of state laws. All information here comes from one or the other of the two websites given above.[21]

Currently, New Jersey requires that guns in vehicles be unloaded and locked in the trunk separately from the ammunition. If you have no trunk, the gun must be "securely tied or fastened."

Florida requires that the gun be kept in a "closed container," but allows guns in cars to be loaded. A "container" includes everything from a cigar box with its lid down to the glove compartment of the vehicle.

Minnesota requires that the gun be unloaded and in a "closed and fastened case, gun box or securely tied package" but does not require that the container be in any particular part of the vehicle. (The vehicle can be a boat or snowmobile, by the way.)

South Dakota, like Minnesota, does not specify where in a vehicle the container must be. South Dakota does, however, require the container to be not only closed, but also too large to be concealed under clothing. Whether that means the clothing must be worn at the time is not specified. Presumably, a 270-pound man in a parka would be able to conceal a far larger container than 105-pound girl in cutoffs and a T-shirt. Does this affect the required size of the container? Does South Dakota have an established one-size-that's-too-big-for-anybody container? It's not clear from the way the law is written, but there may have been rulings. Contact your state Attorney General's office for clarification on such matters.

In Missouri law, "It is unlawful to carry concealed upon or about his person a firearm, a blackjack, or any other weapon capable of lethal use." What is "on or about a person"? Generally, courts around the country

---

[21] www.packing.org

have said that "on or about a person" means that it is within "easy reach and convenient control." But "This prohibition does not apply to transporting a firearm in a nonfunctioning state or in an unloaded state when ammunition is not readily accessible, or while in possession of an exposed firearm . . . for the lawful pursuit of game, or to a person in his dwelling unit or upon business premises over which he has possession, authority or control, or while traveling in a continuous journey peaceably through the state."

As noted earlier, most states have "peaceable journey" laws regarding firearms being transported through the state when the person is bound for some other place. Some states are more lenient about "peaceable journey" than others, provided you do not stop there. From the above, you can see the value of not only knowing the law, but asking for an interpretation from the state's Attorney General's office.

Another source of reliable information is firearms instructors in your state. (The publishers of this book, the American Association of Certified Firearms Instructors, always provide their instructors and students with up-to-date gun laws for their respective states.)

## Unreliable sources

Many people *think* they know the law in your state and will make pronouncements about just how the gun must be transported. "The gun and the ammo have to be at opposite ends of the car," one will say, adding, "I heard that from a cop."

To repeat, you should check the actual law. As with every other subject in the world, people who recite gun laws are often not as well-informed as they think they are. They may have out-of-date information, or may simply be flat-out incorrect. (The likelihood that any state requires a gun be kept in the engine compartment if the ammunition is in the trunk seems very remote.)

## If stopped by the police

If you transport a firearm intelligently, you are unlikely ever to have to discuss it with the police.

Do not lie to the police, but don't volunteer information either. If you are pulled over for rolling through a stop sign, for example, there's no reason to mention that you have a gun in the car. The subject is very unlikely to come up.

If for some reason the police officer asks if you have a gun — usually in the form of the question, "Any guns or drugs in the car?" — you should answer truthfully. "Yes, officer, I have an unloaded gun in a box on the back seat. What do you want me to do?"

Do *not* attempt to show the firearm to him or her, even though that might seem like a helpful, polite thing to do. To a police officer, anyone reaching for a gun is an extreme threat.

Here's a true story. A friend of the author's was serving as a police officer in Arkansas. He stopped a woman for failing to signal a turn. She was driving a car with Florida plates. The officer, who was previously a policeman in Florida, knew that Florida allows people to carry guns in glove boxes, a fact that helped save the woman's life.

He asked to see her license and registration. Without thinking, she reached into the glove box to get her license, forgetting that she also had a gun in there. She grabbed the gun by the grip to move it out of the way. In the next split second, the officer had drawn his revolver, a .357 Magnum. "I had the hammer back and the muzzle to her head," he later said.

He might well have shot the woman, had he not known about Florida law, and had he not also sized her up as someone unlikely to be a criminal. Incidentally, she was violating Arkansas law. He let her go, warning her not to keep the gun there in Arkansas.

The moral of this story is simple: don't reach for a gun, even unintentionally, when talking to the police. Just leave it there and let them tell you what to do. (What the Florida woman should have done was to say, "The license and registration are in the glove box, but there's also a gun in there. What do you want me to do?")

## Transporting by air

It is legal to travel by air with a handgun, although not in your carry-on luggage. Remember, you must also be legally allowed to possess a handgun in your destination. Arriving with a handgun in New York City, Washington, D.C, or the like may very well end in your arrest within minutes of picking up your luggage. Look up your destination's laws at www.nraila.org or www.packing.org.

The gun must be unloaded and in a locked container inside your luggage. When you check in, tell the ticket agent that you are checking a handgun. If the agent is unaware that it's legal, ask for a supervisor. You will have to fill out a form, which will go inside the luggage. The airline will likely direct you to TSA to verify the handgun is unloaded and inside a qualifying case. Ammunition generally must be in a separate container (within the same piece of luggage).

Travel by air with a firearm is not an issue, but be sure to check with the airline for any "unique" requirements they may have.

Do not allow anyone to place a tag on the outside of a suitcase saying there's a gun inside, or the suitcase is likely to be stolen. Any such tag goes *inside* the suitcase. Be polite, but be absolutely insistent.

If luggage needs to be checked through to another airplane, you must not take possession of it in the secured area of the airport. Being in possession of a handgun in such circumstances is a felony. Ask for a supervisor if need be. Ask for the airport police to carry it if need be.

Safety and common sense should be your guiding principles in owning, storing, and transporting a handgun. Understanding the laws in your state and the states to which you travel only makes sense and provides you with a sense of confidence. Additionally, if you were to be caught doing something illegal, law enforcement is likely to be much more understanding if they know you were trying to follow the law.


*And remember - Safety is your responsibility.*

# APPENDIX A
## Anatomy of a Handgun

The diagrams shown in this appendix are used with the permission of, and thanks to, Smith & Wesson.

*Anatomy of a Handgun*

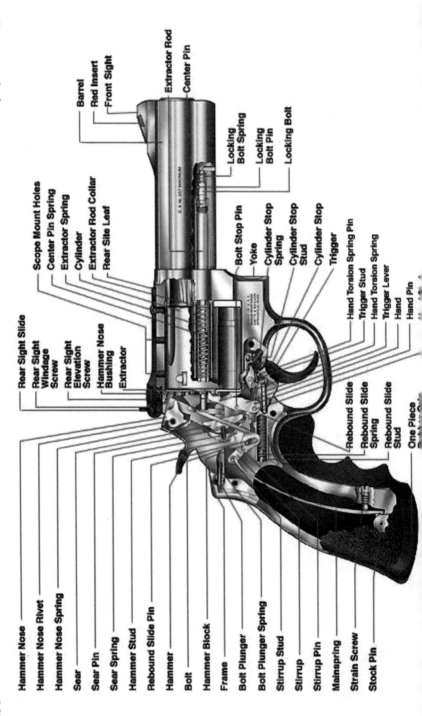

Rear Sight Slide
Rear Sight Windage Screw
Rear Sight Elevation Screw
Hammer Nose Bushing
Extractor

Scope Mount Holes
Center Pin Spring
Extractor Spring
Cylinder
Extractor Rod Collar
Rear Site Leaf

Barrel
Red Insert
Front Sight

Extractor Rod
Center Pin

Locking Bolt Spring
Locking Bolt Pin
Locking Bolt

Bolt Stop Pin
Yoke
Cylinder Stop Spring
Cylinder Stop Stud
Cylinder Stop
Trigger

Hand Torsion Spring Pin
Trigger Stud
Hand Torsion Spring
Trigger Lever
Hand
Hand Pin

Rebound Slide
Rebound Slide Spring
Rebound Slide Stud

One Piece

Hammer Nose
Hammer Nose Rivet
Hammer Nose Spring
Sear
Sear Pin
Sear Spring
Hammer Stud
Rebound Slide Pin
Hammer
Bolt
Hammer Block
Frame
Bolt Plunger
Bolt Plunger Spring
Stirrup Stud
Stirrup
Stirrup Pin
Mainspring
Strain Screw
Stock Pin

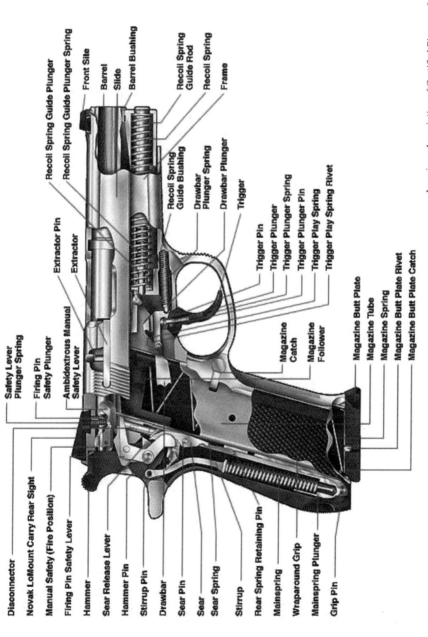

Disconnector
Novak LoMount Carry Rear Sight
Manual Safety (Fire Position)
Firing Pin Safety Lever
Hammer
Sear Release Lever
Hammer Pin
Stirrup Pin
Drawbar
Sear Pin
Sear
Sear Spring
Stirrup
Rear Spring Retaining Pin
Mainspring
Wraparound Grip
Mainspring Plunger
Grip Pin

Safety Lever Plunger Spring
Firing Pin
Safety Plunger
Ambidextrous Manual Safety Lever
Extractor Pin
Extractor

Recoil Spring Guide Plunger
Recoil Spring Guide Plunger Spring
Front Site
Barrel
Slide
Barrel Bushing
Recoil Spring Guide Rod
Recoil Spring
Frame

Recoil Spring Guide Bushing
Drawbar Plunger Spring
Drawbar Plunger
Trigger
Trigger Pin
Trigger Plunger
Trigger Plunger Spring
Trigger Plunger Pin
Trigger Play Spring
Trigger Play Spring Rivet

Magazine Catch
Magazine Follower

Magazine Butt Plate
Magazine Tube
Magazine Spring
Magazine Butt Plate Rivet
Magazine Butt Plate Catch

American Association of Certified Firearms Instructors

# Appendix B
# NRA Safety Rules

The following safety rules are brought to you courtesy of the National Rifle Association (www.nra.org).

## *The fundamental NRA rules for safe gun handling are:*

1. <u>ALWAYS</u> **keep the gun pointed in a safe direction.**
   This is the primary rule of gun safety. A safe direction means that the gun is pointed so that even if it were to go off it would not cause injury or damage. The key to this rule is to control where the muzzle or front end of the barrel is pointed at all times. Common sense dictates the safest direction, depending on different circumstances.

2. <u>ALWAYS</u> **keep your finger off the trigger until ready to shoot.**
   When holding a gun, rest your finger on the trigger guard or along the side of the gun. Until you are actually ready to fire, do not touch the trigger.

3. <u>ALWAYS</u> **keep the gun unloaded until ready to use.**
   Whenever you pick up a gun, immediately engage the safety device if possible, and, if the gun has a magazine, remove it before opening the action and looking into the chamber(s) which should be clear of ammunition. If you do not know how to open the action or inspect the chamber(s), leave the gun alone and get help from someone who does.

## *When using or storing a gun, always follow these NRA rules:*

- **Know your target and what is beyond.**
  Be absolutely sure you have identified your target beyond any doubt. Equally important, be aware of the area beyond your target. This means observing your prospective area of fire before you shoot. Never fire in a direction in which there are people or any other potential for mishap. Think first. Shoot second.
- **Know how to use the gun safely.**
  Before handling a gun, learn how it operates. Know its basic parts, how to safely open and close the action and remove any ammunition from the gun or magazine. Remember, a gun's mechanical safety device is never foolproof. Nothing can ever replace safe gun handling.
- **Be sure the gun is safe to operate.**
  Just like other tools, guns need regular maintenance to remain operable. Regular cleaning and proper storage are a part of the gun's general upkeep. If there is any question concerning a gun's ability to function, a knowledgeable gunsmith should look at it.
- **Use only the correct ammunition for your gun.**
  Only BBs, pellets, cartridges or shells designed for a particular gun can be fired safely in that gun. Most guns have the ammunition type stamped on the barrel. Ammunition can be identified by information printed on the box and sometimes stamped on the cartridge. Do not shoot the gun unless you know you have the proper ammunition.
- **Wear eye and ear protection as appropriate.**
  Guns are loud and the noise can cause hearing damage. They can also emit debris and hot gas that could cause eye injury. For these reasons, shooting glasses and hearing protectors should be worn by shooters and spectators.
- **Never use alcohol or over-the-counter, prescription or other drugs before or while shooting.**
  Alcohol, as well as any other substance likely to impair normal mental or physical bodily functions, must not be used before or while handling or shooting guns.

- **Store guns so they are not accessible to unauthorized persons.**
Many factors must be considered when deciding where and how
to store guns. A person's particular situation will be a major part
of the consideration. Dozens of gun storage devices, as well as
locking devices that attach directly to the gun, are available.
However, mechanical locking devices, like the mechanical safeties built into guns, can fail and should not be used as a substitute for safe gun handling and the observance of all gun safety
rules.
- **Be aware that certain types of guns and many shooting activities require additional safety precautions.**
- **Cleaning**
Regular cleaning is important in order for your gun to operate
correctly and safely. Taking proper care of it will also maintain
its value and extend its life. Your gun should be cleaned every
time that it is used.
A gun brought out of prolonged storage should also be cleaned
before shooting. Accumulated moisture and dirt, or solidified
grease and lubricant, can prevent the gun from operating properly.
Before cleaning your gun, **make absolutely sure that it is
unloaded.** The gun's action should be open during the cleaning
process. Also, be sure that no ammunition is present in the
cleaning area.

# Appendix C
# Interstate Transportation of Firearms

The following text is the US code (Title 18, Part I, Chapter 44, section 926A) as it relates to the interstate transportation of firearms.

"Notwithstanding any other provision of any law or any rule or regulation of a State or any political subdivision thereof, any person who is not otherwise prohibited by this chapter from transporting, shipping, or receiving a firearm shall be entitled to transport a firearm for any lawful purpose from any place where he may lawfully possess and carry such firearm to any other place where he may lawfully possess and carry such firearm if, during such transportation the firearm is unloaded, and neither the firearm nor any ammunition being transported is readily accessible or is directly accessible from the passenger compartment of such transporting vehicle: Provided, That in the case of a vehicle without a compartment separate from the driver's compartment the firearm or ammunition shall be contained in a locked container other than the glove compartment or console."

# APPENDIX D
# Glossary

AACFI researched firearms glossaries for months in hopes of finding a solid glossary we could include in this book. Well, when we found one we really liked, we determined that abridging it or including the entire glossary were both impractical options. So, If you want (what we consider) to be the best firearms glossary please go to SAAMI.org.

# SAAMI.org